the

MODEL
presenter

Developing Excellence in Presenting and Training

Joe Cheal & Melody Cheal

Published in England
by GWiz Publishing
(A division of The GWiz Learning Partnership)
Oakhurst, Mardens Hill, Crowborough, E. Sussex. TN6 1XL
Tel (+44) 1892 309205

info@gwiztraining.com

www.gwiztraining.com

First published 2013.
10 9 8 7 6 5 4 3 2 1

ISBN: 978-0-9548800-5-7

Contents

Acknowledgements

We would like to thank the following people for their help and support along the way:

Graham Browne... *For his wisdom, spirit, intuition, performance, dynamism, challenge and authenticity.*

Julie Silverthorn... *For her elegance, grace, immaculate language patterns, purposeful poise and purposeful application of her craft.*

Tricia Cusden... *For her total professionalism, style, kindness and insightful feedback.*

Keith Crampton... *For his friendship, humour, openness and willingness to give us a 'foot in the door'!*

Every single course participant over the last 20 years... *For their questions, observations, challenges, applications, head-nods, laughter, smiles, 'aha' moments and willingness to learn.*

JC & MC 2013

Foreword

Joe's Foreword

My in front of the audience career began in 1993 when I had a job running week-long workshops for people who had been out of work for more than twelve months. The vast majority of attendees didn't want to be there and to add insult to injury they were told that if they didn't attend the workshop they would lose their income benefits. So, every Monday morning, you can imagine the room full of 'happy bunnies' that we had! It was here that I learnt the art of handling fiery emotions, challenging behaviours and 'difficult people'.

Just before this baptism of fire, I was fortunate enough to experience the most awesome presenter I had ever seen. He was an Australian chap, Graham Browne, who taught a very powerful personal development workshop called the Turning Point. I've never really been a hero worshipper but I thought this guy was amazing as he worked with the audience. He was dynamic, engaging, funny, knowledgeable, profound, clear and inspirational... What a role model! So when I had the job of running week long workshops I stepped into his shoes. I held flip chart pens like he did... I walked around the front of the room like he did... I even had an Australian accent for the first few weeks!

By becoming someone else, I gained the confidence to *be there* at the front of the room. Then within a couple of weeks, I was able to be myself! In reality of course, I didn't *become* someone else... I was still me but I was using someone else's behaviour. It gave me a greater degree of flexibility and most of all it gave me courage. This was one of my first *purposeful* modelling projects.

The Model Presenter

To this day, I love modelling voices. I'm not an impersonator, but I enjoy have a freedom and variety to move around characters and accents. On the odd occasion, however, my love of voices and variety can lead me astray. At the end of one management workshop I ran years ago, a course participant wrote on the feedback form: *"Good course but found the voices a bit off-putting."* Useful feedback but I don't know what his HR Department made of it... what voices was he hearing? On the other hand, I also get feedback like: *"Dynamic, great fun... an excellent combination of Doctor Who and Eddie Izzard!"* Now that's a compliment!

Nearly twenty years after I embarked on a career in presenting and training, I still *love* being in front of the audience. Every group is different and I am forever amused and amazed by people's seemingly infinite capacity for curiosity and desire for solutions. Every group brings new experiences, stories and questions... and with each of these I continue to learn and develop as a presenter and trainer.

Melody's Foreword

I secretly wanted to be an actor. No-one ever found out!

At school I lacked the confidence to put myself forward and ended up being given the job of prompter. I would enviously watch the other children step into the spotlight. I so wanted to do it but I never told a soul.

Things started to look up when I was in the sixth form at school. I was fortunate enough to have a truly inspirational teacher called Liz Fletcher. She was at the start of her career at this point but later went on to become one of the leading head teachers in Sussex. She encouraged me to take the Oxford Certificate in Oral English. This involved reading set classical scripts to an evaluation board. This boosted my confidence somewhat but I was still not acting.

The next step in my journey towards becoming a public speaker was a little unusual. One of my hobbies was training dogs to compete in obedience shows. When I was eighteen I decided to take the British Institute of Professional Dog Trainers Instructors course. There I met Barrie Linford who taught me a great deal about how to motivate and encourage people. Although the goal was dog training the dogs were not the ones we were instructing. I had to learn how to appeal to different types of people and get their attention.

When I returned with my certificate clutched in my eager hand I had a shock to face. I was a member of a small dog training club that had struggled to get members at the beginner level. It had been decided that I would teach the beginner class. So I decided to do something that at that time dog training clubs didn't do. I put an advert in the local paper. Forty people with forty dogs turned up! I had to do some quick thinking. We could only shoe horn twenty in at a time so I split them into two classes. Making myself heard over twenty people and twenty dogs certainly taught me how to manage my voice.

In my early twenties I found myself in a job where I regularly gave presentations to groups of various types from small children to retired people. Engaging these different groups brought many challenges particularly where people were less than interested in the topic I was presenting. I found the best way to engage children was to bring my dog!

At the point that I stepped into becoming a full-time trainer I was fortunate enough to find two excellent models to emulate. The first was Graham Browne, already mentioned in Joe's forward. He really taught me how to bring passion into my training. The second person was Tricia Cusden. She was a corporate trainer who gave Joe and me our first big break by hiring us to work for the big training company she worked for. She actively coached us in how to present in business including providing structured, useful feedback in an inspirational way. As a presenter herself she is poised, elegant and professional. I modelled myself on her to the point of dressing, moving and talking in the same speech patterns she used. These days that might be called stalking!

As I relaxed into my own style I was able to bring my own personality and approach forward, building on the rich background and foundations started by my inspirational school teacher Liz Fletcher.

Introduction

This book is unashamedly a 'how-to' guide. To date, we have both been presenting and training for about twenty years (obviously with breaks in between... that would be far too tiring otherwise). During that time we have discovered many things that work and many things that don't. We have made mistakes and learnt from our mistakes. We have seen others make mistakes and we have learnt from *their* mistakes. But most importantly we have, at times, excelled and we have seen others excel... and we have most definitely learnt from excellence. Our desire is to inspire and share with others *how* to be the best presenters and trainers that they can possibly be.

This book then is based on a twenty year 'informal' modelling project designed to establish what makes the difference between a reasonable presenter and an *excellent* one. We felt it was time to put that modelling project into one written volume. For more information about the project, see Appendix 1.

Presenting and Training

Throughout the book you will see the terms 'presenting' and 'training' and 'presenting/training'. You will also see the terms 'trainer', 'presenter', 'speaker' and 'presenter/trainer'. Most of the book is applicable to both presenting and training although there are a couple of chapters dedicated to each discipline separately. Presenting and Training are two different disciplines; however, most of the skills and solutions of 'communicating to an audience' apply to both.

The Model Presenter

In this book you will find frameworks, ideas, hints and tips that can be applied to a range of presentations and training environments including:

Presentations	Training Environments
• Briefings	• Soft skills development (e.g. people skills, management, leadership and organisational development)
• Information sharing	
• Sales	
• Talks	
• Speeches	• Hard skills development (e.g. legal, IT, HR policy, finance, systems, health and safety)
	• Culture/values facilitation
	• Personal development workshops
	• Teaching seminars
	• Group coaching

About the Book

How the Book is Written

The main focus of the book is 'you', because you are the reader and you presumably want to get as much use out of this book as possible.

We also refer to 'he' and 'she' in examples and 'they' if we are talking about people in general or about a typical person whose gender is unidentified. Sometimes we write very purposely in third person to disassociate issues away from *you* the reader. If you want to know what that's all about, see chapter 8!

You will also find that we talk about ourselves from time to time, perhaps in examples of what we have done or what we have found or what we believe and recommend. You will also find reference to 'I', which could be either one of us. (Imagine that we are both here with you sharing our personal experiences and you will get the idea. You might even be curious as to who is talking at that point!)

Another important point... because this is a 'how to' book we have endeavoured to be very specific, often to the point of giving examples of things you might say in certain situations. It is important that you put these phrases *into your own words*. They are meant as examples... not scripts!

How the Book Works

The book is divided into four parts:

I. The Psychology of Presenting and Training
II. Preparation and Delivery
III. Key Skills for Engaging an Audience
IV. Solutions

Here is an overview of the chapters (which may also give you a bit of a road map if you are looking to prepare and deliver a presentation or training session):

The Model Presenter

Part	Chapter	Overview
I. The Psychology of Presenting and Training	1. The Model	• What is a model presenter? • Qualities, characteristics and behaviours of excellent presenters and trainers.
	2. The Mind of the audience: Closing the Gap	• What is the Mind of the audience? • Closing the psychological gap between yourself and the audience. • Building connection and credibility
	3. Creating a Model Environment: The Psychology of the Room	• What makes a conducive learning environment? • Room set up and layouts. • Media.
II. Preparation and Delivery	4. Preparing Context and Content	• Using the 'BROADCAST' model for preparing material.
	5. Structure: Preparing to Deliver a Presentation	• How to deliver a well structured presentation • Creating a powerful start and finish • Delivering the message
	6. Designing and delivering training courses	• Training styles and learning styles. • Using the 4Mat system • The 'IMPACT' formula
III. Key Skills for Engaging an	7. Body, Voice and Emotion	• Non-verbal congruence • Purposeful body language and voice • The body-voice-emotion connection • Managing emotion in self and others
	8. The Impact of Language	• What does language do to the brain? • Using compelling, flexible and multisensory language • The power of purposeful 'You'

			language • Signposting and meaning making
	9.	Examples, Stories and Metaphors	• The significance of the story • How to tell a meaningful story
IV. Solutions	10.	Handling Questions	• Best practice • Inviting questions • The 'Directions of Thinking' model • Handling challenging questions
	11.	Managing Difficulties	• How presenters create their own difficulties • Working with external difficulties • Handling audience behaviours
	12.	Managing Nerves and Fear: Connecting to Confidence	• Audience Tolerance • Ideas and solutions for handling nerves

The Model Presenter

Chapter 1

The Model

In This Chapter...

In this chapter, you will be introduced to the Model Presenter with an overview of what makes the difference between those who are good and those who are less so. This will be developed into 'Audience/People' and 'Message/Task' oriented qualities and behaviours.

We will be exploring the following questions:

- What is the Model Presenter?
- What is the difference between good and poor presenters?
- What are the qualities of a Model Presenter/Trainer?
- How might you develop these qualities?

What is the Model Presenter?

Since 1993 we have delivered over three thousand days of training between us. In addition, we have attended and observed hundreds of presentations and courses. Some have been excellent and some a little less so. Our curiosity led us to ask 'what makes the difference' and so began an informal long-term modelling project (see Appendix 1).

Taking the best presenters and trainers (and the best of all the rest), we wanted to explore what makes them the best. What do people admire, respect and expect of a presenter/trainer?

The Model Presenter

A simple place to start is looking at people's perceptions of what makes a good and bad presenter/trainer. So we asked a range of groups to come up with their own experiences of presentations and trainings they had attended. Specifically we asked: "What are some of the qualities, characteristics and behaviours of good and bad presenters and trainers?" We also asked them to write down their own reactions to the good and the bad. Whilst this is not an exhaustive list, the table below gives an indication of some of the groups' perceptions.

Table 1a: Groups experiences of good and bad presenters/trainers and the groups reactions.

	Poor Presenters	Good Presenters
Qualities of Presenter	✗ Boring, monotonous ✗ Bullying ✗ Light on content ✗ Lets things get out of control, strays ✗ Doesn't deal with issues raised ✗ Doesn't handle problem people ✗ Patronising ✗ Puts people on the spot ✗ Picks on people ✗ Talks about themselves too much ✗ Talks too quickly ✗ Acts as if they know the only truth (their answer is THE answer!) ✗ Defensive and argumentative ✗ Puts people down ✗ Egotistical	✓ Clear ✓ Engaging ✓ Knowledgeable (broad and deep) ✓ Supportive ✓ Listens ✓ Adapts to group ✓ Covers expected material AND what people want/need ✓ Treats group as adults ✓ Honest ✓ Encourages ✓ Helps people make links to what they already know ✓ Makes information relevant to the group ✓ Respects people's points of view

	Poor Presenters	Good Presenters
Audience Reactions	❖ Switch off ❖ Want to be elsewhere ❖ Don't understand (or care!) ❖ Feel belittled, disrespected ❖ Angry ❖ Distrustful ❖ Don't learn or gain anything from it.	❖ Learn! And want to learn more ❖ Have fun – enjoy ❖ Make connections ❖ Apply what I learn ❖ Respect the trainer ❖ Want to see/hear the trainer again!

The key learning point for the groups who came up with the data in the table above was that:

an audience will become a reflection of the presenter/trainer.

Some presenters and trainers want to blame their audience for being unreceptive. As you can see from the table above, it is often the case that an audience is simply reacting to the presenter. Model presenters on the other hand seem to understand that they have an impact on their audience and that an audience will tend to reflect back the mood and behaviour of the speaker. With enough time, a good presenter can turn a difficult group around.

Qualities of the Model Presenter/Trainer.

If we now dig a little deeper into the good presenter/trainer, how might we categorise some of the key qualities to begin to make a 'model'. From all the data we gathered, we created a structure to people's expectations of a model presenter with example competencies and behaviours. Please note that this will not include everything and may not always account for certain individual differences. For example, there may be some audience members who *like* being talked to without having to get involved in doing things. We all have our own unique map of the world; however, we are working with the majority here.

The following categories appear to cover many of the key qualities of the model presenter/trainer:

Audience/People Oriented Qualities	*Message/Task Oriented Qualities*
Engaging	Professional
Motivational	Practical
Flexible	Structured

And here are some examples of the qualities and behaviours in each category:

	Qualities	Example Behaviours
	Audience/People Oriented Qualities	*Audience/People Oriented Behaviours*
Engaging	• Entertaining • Inclusive • Animated • Interesting • Fun • Humorous • Light hearted • Playful	• Builds rapport with the group • Uses open body language • Makes eye contact with the audience • Smiles often and genuinely • Laughs with the audience • Tells relevant stories as examples • Involves the group in activities and discussions • Draws information from the group • Enjoys being in front of the group

Motivational	• Inspirational • Connected to values/vision • Purposeful • Enthusiastic • Dynamic • Positive • Upbeat • Passionate about the subject	• Uses positive outcome oriented language • Uses purposeful body language • Speaks clearly • Demonstrates passion through emphasis, volume and pitch • Builds energy • Shares their vision
Flexible	• Adaptable to environment/context • Able to read audience and improvise • Sensitive to group mood/needs • Able to be wrong/mistaken • Open to change • Creative • Helpful • Intuitive	• Changes mode of delivery as required • Changes content level for the audience • Asks and answers questions in different ways • Stops to explain jargon if required • Acknowledges any mistakes made • Checks group responses • Notices body language of the group • Uses a variety of activities and exercises • Uses a range of media (visual, auditory & kinaesthetic)

	Message/Task Oriented Qualities	*Message/Task Oriented Behaviours*
Professional	• Accurate • Confident • Authentic • Integrous • Reliable • Consistent • Constructive • Tidy	• References others' work/ materials • Projects a confident image through voice and body language • Understands and respects what the audience has signed up for • Talks openly about own feelings and mistakes as well as successes • Shows up and is ready on time • Delivers agreed material/outcomes

The Model Presenter

Practical	• Factual • Pragmatic • Grounded • Evidence based • Believable • Credible • Detailed • Realistic	• Gives real world examples • Back up statements with evidence • Breaks processes into manageable chunks • Provides handouts with actionable steps • Distinguishes fact from opinion • Suggests applications of the material
Structured	• Clear • Organised • Prepared • Logical • Time aware • Easy to follow • Focussed • Orderly	• Sequences their content into a logical order • Gives an overview of what will be covered • Keeps an eye on the time • Sticks to the allocated time-slot • Signposts throughout the presentation/training • Provides clear explanations

Pick some key qualities that you would like to develop (more of). For each quality consider the following questions:

- What would you get by developing that quality?
- What would developing that quality give your audience?
- Having that quality, how would you behave? What would you do/say?
- How else would you know you have that quality? What would you see, hear and feel?
- How would others know you have that quality?
- Where might you develop that quality?
- How might you develop that quality?

Model Making

As a model presenter:

- Seek to be engaging, motivational, flexible, professional, practical and structured
- Understand that the audience will reflect back some of your feelings and behaviours
- Continue to develop your skills as a presenter/trainer

The Model Presenter

Chapter 2

The Mind of the Audience: Closing the Gap

In This Chapter...

In this chapter, we will be revealing two important concepts: the 'mind of the audience' and 'closing the gap'. You will discover how to close the psychological gap between yourself and the audience so that you can move *from* 'me and them' *to* 'us together'. This will lead to a range of ideas on how to build connection and credibility and how to engage the audience.

We will be exploring the following questions:

- What is the 'mind of the audience'?
- How do you model an audience?
- What does it mean to 'close the gap' and how do you do it?
- How do you build connection and credibility?
- How do you engage an audience?

Modelling the Mind of the Audience

Many, if not most, presenters and trainers start by thinking about what they want to tell/teach the audience. They start with the business need and the content, focussing on the information and message they want to deliver. However, if a presenter leaves it at that, what is the point of the audience being there? If we don't think about the audience themselves then what are we *really* delivering and why? Are we delivering the presentation/training simply because we have been told to?

Plainly put, what happens if we don't know (and hence don't connect) with the audience? In the first instance, we may be pitching information at the wrong level and hence the material may seem boring, disconnected and unprepared. We may then end up with an audience that is (or becomes) unreceptive and/or actively hostile! As discussed in chapter 11, some trainers create their own difficult audiences.

What do we mean by 'modelling the audience'?

Modelling the audience means being able to 'get into' the mind of the audience and understanding how it works. Modelling the audience means closing the psychological gap between the audience and yourself as the speaker. Modelling the audience means knowing the following:

- Who is in the audience?
- Who are they there for? Do they want to be there? What is their overall mood? How open/receptive are they likely to be? How do/might they behave?
- What is their role? What do they already know? What interests them?
- What are their thinking patterns? How do they prefer to take in information? How might they filter the message?
- How do/might they perceive you? Do they know you already? Do they trust you? How much rapport do they feel that they have with you?

Modelling the audience is a process that helps us to understand and connect with the audience and this, in turn, helps the audience to trust and respect us.

The Mind of the Audience

Everyone has their own unique model of the
world. People bring different experiences,
memories, beliefs, values, ideas and
perspectives. An audience is a collection of
people who each have a mind of their own.
However, when a room full of individual
personalities come together they create a
group personality or 'group-mind'. This
group mind, i.e. the mind of the audience,
will sometimes behave differently to the
individuals, like a gestalt, becoming more
than the sum of its parts.

When presenting, training and selling, treat the group mind as if it
is already 'full'. Imagine that it doesn't need anything from you (or
at least doesn't know that it does!) and that it is content with the
status quo (even if the current situation is not pleasant). As far as
the group mind is concerned, it knows everything it needs to know.
So, in order to add something to the mind of the audience, you will
need to create a space first in which your proposal can sit. What
creates a space? Here a few examples:

- An overt and acknowledged dissatisfaction with how things
  are currently,
- Confusion and doubt about the current state,
- A feeling of purposelessness in the current state,
- The concern about an unpleasant future if things continue
  the same way.

It is important that as soon as you have created a space in the mind
of the audience that you give them the benefits and purpose of what
you are sharing with them. You do not want the group mind feeling
negative for too long.

The Model Presenter

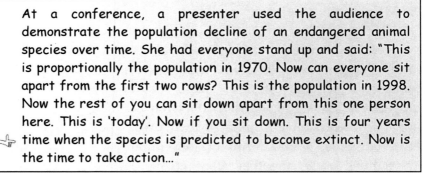

A Case In Point

At a conference, a presenter used the audience to demonstrate the population decline of an endangered animal species over time. She had everyone stand up and said: "This is proportionally the population in 1970. Now can everyone sit apart from the first two rows? This is the population in 1998. Now the rest of you can sit down apart from this one person here. This is 'today'. Now if you sit down. This is four years time when the species is predicted to become extinct. Now is the time to take action..."

Research around conformity and 'social validation' (e.g. see Robert Cialdini's book 'Influence'[1]) suggests that individuals who have identified with the group will sometimes act outside their normal range of behaviours. It is as if the group mind gives the individuals permission to be 'other than themselves'. The pull of the group can be seductive... "I wouldn't normally have done that but others were doing it so I just joined in".

The group mind will sometimes act like fire, spreading suddenly across a room, either in agreement with an individual (speaker or audience member), or in dissent. A quiet group can be sparked off by one toxic comment or soothed by a voice of reason. It can split into factions and become conflicted (known as the problem of *disagreement*). Alternatively it can develop what Irvin Janis[2] called 'groupthink' where no-one is prepared to speak up (known as the problem of *agreement*).

Sometimes it is useful to be considered part of the group mind, as if 'we are all in it together'. However, sometimes you might need to be *outside* the group mind, acting as an expert or consultant to the group.

Fortunately, the group-mind responds well to people it trusts and likes. If someone has authority and rapport with the group, they are usually in a good place to deliver their message. The first step in gaining the trust and heart of the group-mind is to 'close the gap'...

Closing the Gap: Into the Mind of the audience

A Case In Point

It is the stuff of bad dreams... the presenter stands alone in silence. He or she cracks a joke to 'warm up the crowd'... but nothing. No reaction but an embarrassed cough. From out of no-where it seems that a breeze has kicked up and tumble weed blows across the increasing gap. Nerves are on edge, mouth is dry and mind goes blank. It is a surreal sensation as the presenter searches frantically for words... any words. Instead of any sensible response, the brain disengages and the presenter feels like they are about a million miles away from their body... watching themselves though a distorting lens of quiet desperation...

Whilst we hope this doesn't sound too familiar to you personally, it is a culmination of how people have described their experience of being in front of an audience. So how do we prevent this 'nightmare' scenario?

Key Pointer

Confidence comes from closing the psychological gap between yourself and the audience.

Throughout the book you will see the phrase 'close the gap'. We believe that one of the main reasons for nerves and lack of engagement is a psychological gap between the presenter and the audience. It is the job of the presenter to close this gap.

A psychological gap between the presenter and audience may result in the audience switching off. Of course, the gap might have something to do with the mood and state of the audience but it is even more about the presenter and their own state. By closing the gap and knowing that a group will find what you have to say interesting, this will help you feel more confident and enthusiastic.

The Model Presenter

From the outset, whilst preparing a presentation, you can begin to close the gap (even before you have the audience in front of you). Then, when you get to the place of presenting and the audience gathers, you can continue to close the gap before you have said a word! Then, through your introduction and beyond, you can continue to close the gap until, psychologically, it feel like you are all 'on the same side'... you are in harmony with the audience and it is as if you are all working together in making something useful happen... a common aim... a shared purpose.

Some presenters will teach, talk and preach at an audience, pushing information, acting as an expert imparting knowledge. They have information to give out and the audience might as well not be there. The focus for this type of presenter is *information*. They ask questions like: "What do I want to tell them? What do I want them to know and do? What is the best way for me to share my information with them?" Whilst it is admirable that they are at least thinking of how to get their message across to the audience, you will find it more helpful to work the other way round.

When you are communicating *with* the group, the best way to close the gap is to work *from* the mind of the audience *to* your message rather than *vice versa*. When you start with the audience in mind, you are more likely to be *in* the mind of the audience. At this point, you are going to be presenting/training from the audience's map of the world rather than from your own. You will use their metaphors and give examples related to their immediate experience...

You know what it's like when a presenter or trainer stands at the front of the room and lectures at you, perhaps about things you know already or don't really care about. Have you ever wondered whether that person is really all that bothered about the audience or even wants to be there themselves? As a communicator, when you close the gap and step into the mind of the audience, you will find that your audience is more likely to care about what you have to say.

Model presenters present from the mind of the audience. Although information is obviously important, the primary focus is the audience. When preparing, they ask questions like:

- What are the audience already likely to know? What do they want to know?
- What do they do? What job do they have?
- What is their likely experience of the things I am going to be talking about?
- How can my material be related to what they know and do?
- How might I use their experiences to give examples of what I'm talking about?
- When they have this information, how will this help them?

To close the gap, use examples and stories that relate to the group. Use any connected experiences they may have had. For example, on an 'introduction to management' course, not everyone will necessarily be a manager already, but they *will* have all been managed... hence they have experience of 'management'.

To explore the concept of closing the gap further, there are two key things we have discovered that a presenter/trainer needs in order to engage the mind of the audience. They need to make sure they have connection with the audience (i.e. that the audience feel an empathy and rapport with) and credibility (i.e. that the audience feel that they are knowledgeable and trustworthy).

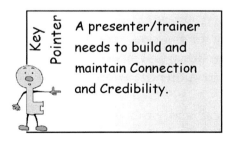

Key Pointer

A presenter/trainer needs to build and maintain Connection and Credibility.

When in front of the audience, until you build connection and credibility, there will tend to be a sense of separation from the group-mind. There may be times when this is necessary perhaps, but it is generally more desirable to step into the mind of the audience and close the gap.

Connection and Credibility: The Keys to Closing the Gap

When you are liked and trusted by the audience your job becomes so much easier and, depending on the content/message, much more enjoyable. With connection and credibility, you tend to experience less resistance from the audience because they have less need to object (to you personally or to your message).

Losing the Mind of the Audience: How to Destroy Credibility and Connection!

Before we explore ways that you can build connection and credibility with a group, we will first look at what doesn't normally work. In our modelling quest, as well as finding best practice, we have also discovered how presenters destroy their credibility and connection with an audience. We couldn't resist putting this section in the book as a word of warning. Obviously the following are behaviours to avoid... unless you want a new and different experience. We have observed presenters and trainers creating a chasm between themselves and the audience by doing such things as:

- Disagreeing strongly with the audience, pointing at the audience, telling them 'no' and/or making them wrong. Being unsupportive if the audience doesn't respond as expected. Asking for input and then seeking a specific answer... and then dragging that specific answer out of the audience!
- Picking on people in the audience for answers... encouraging the audience to regress back to the worst aspects of the school classroom. Embarrassing an audience member if they can't answer or get it 'wrong'.
- Being constantly negative, cynical and problem focussed. Disrespecting the audience, making the lack of receptiveness the fault of the audience and accusing them of such: "What's the matter with you lot then?" Disrespecting the company,

project or competition... indeed anyone other than themselves.

- Belittling themselves and/or their message... saying things like: "I won't bore you with the details"
- Using lots of jargon and TLAs without explaining them (that would be Three Letter Abbreviations by the way!) and without gauging the audience. Using 'big' and/or complex words without defining them with a simple one sentence definition or metaphor.

Consider how you might react to some of the above if you were in the audience!

Now let us move on to what works...

<u>Building and Maintaining Connection</u>

Connection can be built and maintained in numerous ways:

- *Empathy*: The audience feel that the speaker cares about them and their concerns. In turn, the audience feel some empathy for the speaker. The speaker likes them and so they like the speaker. They also feel that the speaker *is* like them; on the same side and hence part of the team.
- *Enthusiasm*: The audience feel that the speaker has a passion for their subject.
- *Fun*: The audience feel that the speaker is entertaining and makes the subject enjoyable. The speaker makes them laugh and smile.
- *Fitting-in*: The audience feel that the speaker is 'on their wavelength,' sharing their culture and values. They have the same goals, vision and purpose in mind and they are engaging because they fit their message to the expectations,

experience and requirements of the audience.

- *Reassurance*: The audience feel that they are in kind and capable hands and that everything is going to be okay.
- *Involvement*: The audience feel engaged by the speaker and that they are part of the presentation/training. They feel like participants rather than observers. The speaker asks questions and listens to the answers.
- *Acknowledgement*: The audience feel that the speaker complements them and appeals to their skills and expertise. The speaker doesn't come across as patronising or condescending.

Building and Maintaining Credibility

Credibility can be built and maintained in numerous ways:

- *Authority*: The audience perceive that the speaker knows their subject. The speaker is considered to be an expert and experienced in their field.
- *Qualified*: The audience perceive that the speaker has qualifications linked to the subject.
- *Trust*: The audience perceive that the speaker is truthful and is able to predict and handle situations effectively.
- *Confidence*: The audience perceive that the speaker has the courage of their convictions. The speaker comes across with certainty.
- *Professionalism*: The audience perceive that the speaker is reliable, smart and keeps to time.
- *Accuracy*: The audience perceive that the speaker's information is clear, believable and correct.
- *Grounded*: The audience perceives that the speaker is pragmatic and working in the 'real world'. The speaker gives concrete evidence and references to back up what they are saying. Their solutions are workable and their advice is solid.

The trick with connection and credibility is to find the balance. Too much connection can feel overly familiar (which ironically breaks connection) and too much credibility can feel patronising or condescending (which ironically breaks credibility... and connection). Connection without credibility results in 'nice but untrustworthy'. Credibility without connection results in (at best) 'compliance without commitment'.

Ultimately, if the audience does not feel a connection with the speaker or does not perceive that the speaker is credible, there is a risk of the message becoming lost.

Humour is an interesting case in point since although it can develop connection it rarely develops credibility. When it is used for credibility it tends to break connection! Some presenters try using humour to make themselves look (and feel) better by using put-downs and 'one-upmanship'. Making someone else the butt of the joke may be funny to some but it rarely builds friends. An overuse of humour (without enough other sources of credibility) makes the speaker seem like a clown... amusing but not someone you would take advice from.

Whilst this section has looked at the 'what' you need as a speaker (i.e. connection and credibility), the next section will look at the 'how' (i.e. ways of engaging the audience).

Engaging the Audience: Push and Pull

Presenting from the Mind of the audience may mean sharing information and sometimes teaching or briefing (i.e. pushing information), but it will also mean gathering information from the group (i.e. pulling information). The model presenter works out which approach is the most appropriate given the audience's knowledge, experience, and motivation. However, even when pushing information, this is still driven by the perspective, needs and expectations of the audience.

Pushing information means talking to the group and giving direction. As the speaker, you are giving out information and sharing your experience with the audience. Pulling information is usually more non-directive; it is about asking questions and listening to the experience of the group. As with credibility and connection there is a need to balance pushing and pulling. Too much push is the old style 'talk and chalk' teacher. Too much pull and the speaker begins to lack credibility (unless their brief is purely to facilitate).

Pushing and pulling are two ends of a continuum. The general rule of thumb is: the less experienced/knowledgeable the group is about a specific topic, the more you may have to push. Then the more experienced/knowledgeable they are the more you pull. Pushing to an experienced group will be teaching them to 'suck eggs'. Pulling at a group who are inexperienced will be like 'pulling teeth'. As a presenter/trainer, you will know whether you are using the right or wrong approach by the reaction you get!

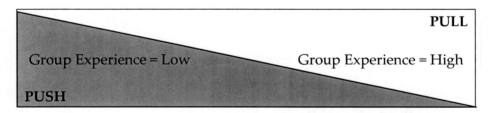

How to Push

- *Give examples*: Concrete evidence is useful in adding credibility whilst personal anecdotes can make a point whilst building connection. Examples can be about other people you know or how certain companies do things. The nature of examples and stories are explored in more detail in chapter 9.

- *Share benefits*: Have you ever been to a presentation and thought "why am I here? How is this relevant to me?" By thinking about the benefits to the audience, you can tell them in your introduction: "by the end of this presentation you will know how to X or be able to Y." If you can't think of a benefit to the audience then how are they meant to? Every presentation is about moving the hearts and minds of an audience. Benefits are about how to get the audience on board (rather than how to get them bored!)

- *Refer to the audience*: By linking your message to the audience as a group (or to individuals in the group) it demonstrates knowledge of who people are and what they do. When that link is complimentary (e.g. to the expertise of an individual or the achievement of the organisation), this helps to build connection and credibility. Reference can also be made to previous comments and questions made by the audience.

- *Use inclusive language*: When you talk in terms of 'we' (as in you *and* the audience) you are linguistically suggesting that you are part of the group and 'in it together'. When you talk in terms of 'you' (as opposed to 'it') this will help the audience to associate to your topic. For more on this see chapter 8.

- *Use purposeful body language and voice*: Make it easy for the audience to watch and listen to you. Make eye contact around the audience, smile and use your voice range. This will be explored in more detail in chapter 7.

- *Tell anecdotes*: Relating stories about your own experience can allow you to build connection and credibility. Let the audience know what you did, why you did it and why you liked it! Avoid too many stories however, unless you are doing a stand up comedy routine or a memoire.

How to Pull

- *Invite questions from the audience*: Where appropriate and possible, allow the audience to ask questions and make comments on what you are discussing. See chapter 10 on handling questions for more information.
- *Gauge the experience of the group*: You might ask the group, for example, "Can I just get a show of hands... how many of you are familiar with X?" or "How many of you have done X?" This allows the audience to acknowledge their experience and lets you know who knows what (or at least who *believes* they know what!)
- *Invite interactivity*: Make it a two way process, encourage participation and ensure group understanding. One of the best ways to learn as a trainer is to let the group add their own experiences, concerns, challenges and solutions.
- *Invite and utilise volunteers from the audience*: When appropriate it can be fun to invite someone from the audience to participate in a demonstration or help you explain something. Make sure you thank them as you ask them to return to their seats and give them a round of applause (inviting the audience to join in).
- *Elicit associations with a word, phrase or concept to gauge the group*: Sometimes it is useful to gauge how an audience is thinking and feeling about a particular topic. For example, on a change management course, by asking people: "What do you associate with 'Change'... what springs to mind?" or "What are three words you associate with change?" you can get an understanding as to whether people are feeling in a good place, bad place or mixed about it. It will also give you an indicator if there is an individual who is in a different place to others in the audience.
- *Get the group talking to each other*: Use subgroups to break the audience into smaller chunks. Some people don't like speaking up in front of the whole audience, but they will happily do so with three or four others. Then someone else

can be the spokesperson in the main group when debriefing. As long as the audience has some knowledge, experience and opinions you can use subgroups to get the audience:

- o Coming up with ideas (e.g. examples or suggestions)
- o Answering 'quiz' questions (to check knowledge or have them find out information from a source)
- o Sharing experiences (e.g. real world examples of issues or successes)
- o Considering solutions to situations and/or case studies (e.g. how would they deal with X or handle situation Y?)

- *Ask the group questions*: Invite the audience to input...

Asking Questions: Inviting the Audience to Input

Surprisingly, this is one area that presenters and trainers seem to make mistakes. Indeed, the test of a model presenter/trainer is not necessarily the questions the audience asks them, but the questions they ask the audience. The challenge here can be the answers that the audience gives! When you ask a question of the audience, be prepared for their responses...

o *Answers that don't fit with what you are looking for.* Some trainers appear to want specific answers from the group and so they drag it out until they get what they are looking for. This can be frustrating for the audience and gives the appearance of an inflexible trainer. If you are using a flipchart – write down their answers as they say it, i.e. *using their words.* If you are looking for a specific answer (e.g. "X") and you get something similar from the audience, write down what is said and then subtly interpret it and/or draw a likeness (e.g. "this is kind of like X") or a link (e.g. "an example of this might be X").

o *Late answers and quiet answers.* A shy person being brave might answer the question quietly and hence get overlooked. This may lead them to lose confidence and so not say anything else.

The Model Presenter

Sometimes the audience will tell you, so thank the audience and apologise to the person you missed!

o *No answers.* Give the group time to answer and avoid answering the question yourself. If there is silence, rephrase the question or give an example. For example, the question: "what is motivation?" might be rephrased to "what is motivation *to you?*" If there is no answer, you might say: "If I was to say 'being positive' what would you add to that?"Sometimes it is good practice to ask a question in different ways to engage the audience into answering. E.g. "What wastes your time? How is your time wasted? How do others waste your time? How might you waste your own time?"

As a final note on asking questions: avoid asking a question to one specific unsuspecting person. It may come across as if you are picking on people and they will invariably feel like they are back at school!

Model Making

As a model presenter:
- Create some variety for the audience... mix it up a little
- Step into the mind of the audience
- Seek to close the gap between yourself and the audience
- Build and maintain connection and credibility with the audience

Chapter 3

Creating a Model Environment:
The Psychology of the Room

In This Chapter...

In this chapter, we will be covering some of the key elements of how to create an environment that is conducive to receptiveness and learning. We will provide an overview of different room layouts and some tips on using a variety of media.

We will be exploring the following questions:

- What is a Model Environment?
- How can you create an engaging venue and room?
- What is the psychological impact of room layout?
- What are some of the pros and cons of different media?

The Model Environment

A Case In Point

The presenter stands at the front of the room, speaking with passion about their subject. They are in flow and in the zone. It is a shame that the audience are finding it hard to pay attention. The subject is fine and the speaker is engaging enough. However, there is a buzzing noise coming from a fluorescent light which flickers every so often. The room is a little cold and the chairs are not exactly comfortable. Added to that, the speaker has been talking for a while and there hasn't been a break...

The Model Presenter

Does the environment affect the 'mind of the audience'? Of course it does! It doesn't have to be the most lavish, luxurious environment but it does need to be comfortable, practical and functional. Back in 1943, Abraham Maslow[1] presented a 'hierarchy of needs' and suggested that if the lower needs are not being met, it will make it more difficult for people to focus on the higher needs. The lower needs include physiological comfort and feeling of safety and security. Once the basic needs are met, people can begin to focus on their social needs, self esteem needs and self actualisation. Frederick Herzberg[2] simplified this in the 1950s by suggesting that there are motivators and 'hygiene' factors. We have developed this into 'motivators' and 'satisfiers' (as we believe that satisfaction is not the same as motivation).

Using Herzberg's principles, if motivators are in place, people feel motivated (i.e. uplifted or feeling some sense of momentum). If motivators are not in place, there is 'no motivation' (i.e. a neutral or perhaps boring experience). If satisfiers are in place, people feel satisfied (i.e. a sense of 'good', 'okay', 'complete', 'comfortable'), but if they are not in place, there is a sense of 'demotivation' (i.e. actively unhappy, uncomfortable and dissatisfied). If satisfiers are not in place, it is hard for people to be actively engaged and motivated to learn. In this sense, satisfiers are the platform on which motivation sits. In the training room, the environment provides a significant chunk of the satisfiers.

Something else to be aware of... today's motivators are tomorrow's expectations. Satisfiers 'oil the wheels' but soon get taken for granted. Once people get used to the chocolate biscuits at break times, there will be hell to pay if there are none supplied later!

If the satisfiers are not right for an audience, they will usually end up focussing on those things (i.e. what is not right). They may get grumpy and awkward. It is up to the trainer/presenter to make the best of the environment, apologise for things that are not right and do whatever they can to put things right. In addition, they need to be reading the behaviours of the individuals in the audience. Who is expressing signs of being cold? Who is expressing signs of being uncomfortable? Who is expressing signs of being confused or puzzled? In addition, they will need to be reading the Mind of the audience. What is the general mood? Who is speaking more and who has gone quiet?

Because the environment affects the mind of the audience, the rest of this chapter will give you some ideas of what to check and look out for...

The Venue

If you are familiar with (or have some control of) the venue and the layout, all well and good. If not, find out and put in your request for it to be set up the way you need it. In addition, put yourself in the mind of the audience... what do people need to know about the venue and what do they want when they get there?

Here are some venue questions that people tend to have when attending a course or presentation:

- *Location/Transport*: Where is it? How do I get there? Where is the car parking?
- *Access*: How easy is it to get to and get into? Is there wheelchair access?
- *Facilities*: Where are the toilets? Where is the coffee/tea point? What food is available?
- *Room*: Is there a breakout area or are we in the same room all the time?

The Model Presenter

The Room

Put yourself in the mind of the audience. How would it feel to sit in a chair in this room and listen to someone talking for a while? Would you be able to see and hear the speaker easily? Are you comfortable? Is the lighting good (neither too dim nor too bright)? Is there light shining in your face (e.g. spotlights or sun through window)?

Now look around the room for the audience as a group. How big is the audience and how big is the room? Are there enough chairs or way too many? What are the acoustics like? Will people be able to hear each other? What if someone at the front of an auditorium asks a question... will others hear it?

<u>Room layout</u>

We have found that there are different layouts that work well for different environments and contexts. Some we believe are less effective (no matter how popular!) as they fragment the mind of the audience.

a) U-Shape

 The U-shape is a classic professional training room layout for groups of up to 20 people. Everyone faces in towards the centre and has the comfort and convenience of a table to write at. Everyone can see the trainer, flipchart and screen. The trainer can move into the 'U' without the feeling of 'space invasion' - although too much of this may lose contact with people on the edges. This is our recommended layout for corporate training.

b) Horseshoe

Like the U shape but without tables. This semicircle effect is good for more personal development workshops that are experimental and require less writing and formality.

c) Boardroom

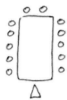

Everyone sits round a table so they can write. This layout is best suited to smaller meetings rather than training. Make sure the person at the other end of the table is an ally; otherwise you may find a dominant character 'stealing' the attention of the group.

d) Theatre

Theatre style is good for presentations and seminars and is for larger groups where everyone faces the front of the room. It makes the best use of room-space and allows each member of the audience to have their own 'privacy' (i.e. no-one else is looking at them). It is important that people don't feel too cramped and that everyone can see the visual aids and make eye contact with the trainer. We recommend that the presenter/trainer has a bar stool for this layout (unless they are on a raised stage already) so they can see everyone. This environment allows the speaker to stand up and move around whilst still being visible.

e) Classroom and Herringbone

Without wishing to appear controversial, this is *not* a layout we would recommend for adult learners. It tends to throw people back into their associations with school... and so they may be compelled to behave like children.

f) Cabaret

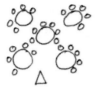 Whilst fashionable, cabaret style doesn't focus the group on the trainer/presenter. This means the presenter must work extra hard to keep the audience's attention. Everybody's focus is towards the table they are sitting at and this can encourage side conversations. The layout may perhaps be good for group work, but it does not aid in the overall speaker-audience dynamic. It can also create clan mentality ('us and them') with other tables, where the whole audience can feel fragmented into cliques and silos. We would tend to avoid this layout whenever possible.

Creating a Multisensory Environment

We are physical creatures and we process information through our five senses. What can you do to make sure that your environment is pleasing to *all* the senses? Obviously, it helps if there are no flickering lights, irritating noises, uncomfortable chairs, extreme temperatures and bad smells... but the absence of these things is hardly outstanding! Here are some ideas to get you started (or to get you starting to think about the audience in a multisensory way):

Visual
(Sight)
- Pleasant pictures/ornaments around the room
- A neutral/easy colour
- Adaptable brightness
- An appropriately dressed presenter!

Auditory
(Sound)
- Quietness
- A speaker with a purposeful voice
- Possibly some appropriate music (though check with copyrights, venue permissions and licences!)

Kinesthetic
(Feeling)
- Comfortable chairs and temperature
- Enough personal space
- Get the group moving around from time to time. Give them something to do.

Olfactory (Smell)	• Get some of the pleasant scented pens (rather than the mind altering 'pear drop' versions)
	• A bit of aromatherapy or fragrant 'reed diffusers'
	• A speaker who smells nice!
Gustatory (Taste)	• Biscuits, sweets, chocolate
	• Fruit

As a general rule, it is worth establishing how much noise you are allowed to make as a group. We have been told off a few times for making too much noise... a couple of which were for people laughing too much. Go figure!

The Media

What media are you using? How easily will it be seen by the audience? Here are some typical media used for delivering training and presentations, along with some pros, cons and tips.

	Pros	Cons	Solutions
Power Point	• Professional • Branded • Supports content of presentation/training • Creates a structure for delivery • Can be used as a prompt • Good for pictures/photos	• Busy slides • Too many slides • Distracting animations • Controls the presenter presentation • Presenter turns back on audience and focuses on screen. • Equipment failure (e.g. incompatibility)	• Bullet points • Key facts/figures • Simple diagrams • Minimal amount of information • Legible – appropriate size writing • Have your laptop in front of you so you don't have to turn back to the screen.

Flip Chart/ Whiteboards Interactive Screens	• You control the content • Interactive • Capturing data • Organic – build pictures • Can be used by participants in exercises/ group-work	• Hard to see for bigger audience • Limited content • Can look untidy/ poor handwriting • Time consuming to capture data • Trainer captures data using own words instead of audience words.	• Use for smaller audience • Write legibly • Prepare diagrams in pencil then trace over with marker pen when delivering
Manuals/ Handouts	• Useful reference for audience. • Information to take away – everyone gets same info. • Provide details. • Use to engage audience • Can be used as a prompt (have your own notes on your copy of the handout)	• Could be distracting if given out part way through • People might read ahead	• Decide when to give out handouts • Put them together as one set (rather than drip feeding one handout at a time) • If there is a massive amount of information, have some of it as a download
Props	• Show real examples – aid understanding • Can be engaging	• Distracting – takes too long to go round group • Props get broken • Encourages side conversations.	• Refer to the prop a number of times to keep it relevant. • Let people take a closer look at the end/ in a break. • Make sure it is not unique/ priceless

From the table above, if the 'pros' of a particular medium (or combination of media) meets your requirement better than others then this may be your best option. Whichever option you choose, be prepared for the cons by having some contingency (back-up) plans in place.

Model Making

As a model presenter:

- Make sure the environment is comfortable and conducive to learning
- Request the room layout that suits your requirements
- Use appropriate visual aids and media to support your message

The Model Presenter

Chapter 4

Preparing Context and Content

In This Chapter...

In this chapter, you will be introduced to the BROADCAST Model which will take you through the key steps in preparing material for a presentation or training session. This will ensure that you have gathered and organised the information in a way that you can deliver it with confidence.

We will be exploring the following questions:

- How do you prepare material for a presentation or training session?
- What is the BROADCAST Model and what are the steps?
- How do you arrange your material so that it is logical, easy to remember and easy to follow?

Modelling Content Preparation

Most presentations and training sessions begin with some ideas and a blank piece of paper. However, before you launch into writing what you want to deliver, you might want to consider the following. Have you ever been to a presentation that:

- Didn't make sense?
- Was hard to follow?
- Jumped around and had no apparent logic?

- Seemed irrelevant to you?
- Failed to keep your interest?
- Made you wonder why you were even there?

In order to avoid the above and to make your own session interesting, engaging and well structured, we would recommend the 'BROADCAST' model as a way of preparing and structuring your material so you feel confident in what you are delivering.

'BROADCAST' Preparation

We developed the BROADCAST model as the first step in 'closing the gap' between yourself and the audience. When preparing to present, have a look at the following stages. They are in a logical sequence but you may want to check back with previous stages as you prepare to ensure that what you are delivering serves the purpose (big picture and reason) of what you wanted to achieve.

B	Big picture
R	Reason
O	Outcome
A	Audience
D	Delivery style/medium
C	Content
A	Arrangement of content
S	Steps
T	Take-aways

We recommend that you consider BROADCAST as a model of two parts. The 'BROAD' part can be covered relatively quickly as long as you are happy that you know the context. The CAST part will take more of your time because it will give you the details of your presentation. At the end of BROADCAST, you should have a clear sequence ready for delivery. Then, depending on whether you are presenting or training, have a look at the next two chapters to put the complete structure together.

1) Big picture

Before getting into the details, stop for a moment and get clear about the big picture. If you are going to deliver a presentation or training, what is the overall context? What situation has led to the need for your presentation/training? What is happening in the organisation, how does your presentation/training 'plug in' to the corporate vision and strategy?

2) Reason

When you understand the context for presenting, you can then clarify the purpose. Why do it? What is the overall purpose of the presentation/training? How might it benefit the team, department, organisation, social group, society or the world? How does it contribute to the success of the organisation?

Depending on your context, you may be seeking to create a positive change at a number of levels, from an individual level to the group, to the system or organisation to society and/or to the world. How does your input benefit at these different levels?

If appropriate, you might also want to consider this question on a personal level. What do *you* get by delivering this presentation/training?

In addition, how will the audience benefit from attending your presentation? What should they be able to do afterwards? What will they know? How will their lives be improved? In every presentation and training you deliver, you will presumably want the audience to *do* something differently as a result. However, as well as wanting to motivate them to do something with your information, you will also want to motivate them to listen to your presentation. Give them a reason to listen to you. How will you move the audience's hearts and minds to get them on board and engaged? If you don't know how your presentation will benefit the audience, how are they expected to? This is one of the differences between an excellent presenter and a mediocre one. A mediocre presenter just delivers the data; the excellent presenter creates a context and a psychological desire for the data before delivering it.

Examples of Benefits

One way to elicit the benefits for the audience is to ask: "What will they get by attending and listening and applying the content of my presentation?" Write a list of whatever comes to mind. Then, go through each item on your list and ask yourself: "So what? What will that give them?"

---

a) Teaching a group a psychological model. As this is a teaching/ training example, it should be easier to establish some 'why':

What will they get? *What will they be able to do?*	*So what?* *What will that give them?*
1. Understand how people think 2. Know why people do what they do 3. Predict which kind of person they are dealing with	1. "By understanding how people think you can build rapport and speak their language. You will be able to solve problems and communicate to them in a way they understand, hence increasing your chances of them agreeing with you." 2. "By knowing why people do what they do, you will be able to empathise more easily and find ways of working with them that reduce the likelihood of conflict." 3. "By predicting what kind of person you are dealing with, you can adapt your approach so that they are more likely to understand and respect you."

b) Presenting updates on a set of figures. In this case the benefits to the audience of such information sharing (as opposed to 'teaching') can sometimes be less obvious to find. Perhaps, however, this makes it even more important to establish the 'why'. Obviously the example below is rather generic but it may give you some ideas:

What will they get? *What will they be able to do?*	*So what?* *What will that give them?*
1. Understand the current status of the business 2. Know which areas are performing well and which are not 3. Use the information to motivate others and/or address issues	1. "By understanding the current status of the business, you can see the bigger picture beyond your own role. This is a useful reminder that we are all in it together in making the organisation successful." 2. "By knowing which areas are working well, you may be able to see patterns and behaviours that are getting us t where we need to be and those that are taking us in another direction." 3. "By using the information to problem solve and motivate, we can get more creative in how get back on track or continue to excel at what we do."

3) Outcome

Every presentation and training needs to have an outcome or set of outcomes. By understanding the objective/outcome, you have something to focus on, something to look towards. What outcome are you seeking to achieve by delivering the presentation/training? What problems are you solving, issues are you addressing, questions are you answering and improvements are you suggesting?

In order to achieve your outcome, what do you want people to know as a result of the presentation? In addition to this, what do you want people to *do* as a result? If nothing changes and people don't do anything differently after attending the presentation/ training, what was the point? Even if it a case of 'sharing information'... for what purpose? What is changing? If the answer is 'nothing', is this the best way to share the information?

By understanding the objective, you will have a better understanding of the scope of your presentation/training, i.e. what is it designed to do and not do and hence what is it designed to cover and not cover?

4) Audience

Some people seem to prefer presenting to a group of strangers whereas others prefer to present to a group they know. So, who are your audience? Do they know you already (in which case you will already have a level of connection and credibility), or not (in which case you will need to build connection and credibility from scratch)?

How many people do you have in the group? Whilst this might not affect the content you want to cover, it may affect your delivery style and medium.

What are the experience levels of the group? When you have a group of novices in the room, it is usually relatively straightforward because you can go back to basics. The challenge is where you have a mix of experience in the group. Some people know a lot but still have to be there and then you have others who know very little. How do you deal with that? How do you keep everybody happy? How do you pitch it? How much jargon can you use without losing half the audience?

It may depend on who makes up the majority of the audience, but here is an idea in terms of the level at which to pitch a presentation/training:

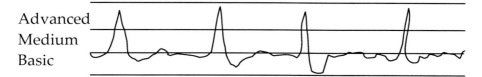

This might mean briefly referencing advanced material from time to time, just to give the audience an indication that you know more than you are generally discussing. It also give the advanced members of the audience some acknowledgement and food for thought whilst helping them make links to what you are talking about (without losing the people who are novices).

When putting your content together, another consideration is how do you want the audience to feel as a result of attending? Do you want them to be curious, interested, excited or perhaps entertained? Remember that these states and feelings do not magically happen by themselves... your delivery will make the difference.

5) Delivery style and medium

Given the big picture, reason, outcome and audience, how do you want to deliver your presentation/training for the best effect? Do you want the more focussed structure of 'power point' slides or the organic, free flow of the flipchart? Does the size of the audience or the layout of the room suggest a particular medium?

The pros and cons of different media were explored in Chapter 3 (along with some tips for usage). Any media that you pre-prepare (e.g. slides, manuals and handouts) will be dependent on the group size, room size, resources available and the content of your presentation.

6) Content

- What do you want to cover?
- What do you want to tell people about?
- What content is inside/outside the scope of the presentation?

The first step is to write out some ideas of what you want cover. At this stage, it can be fairly random, from specific things to general things and in no particular order.

Once you have written out some ideas for your content, show these ideas to one or two other people who might be typical of your audience (or who are familiar with your audience type). Get them to add any questions they might want answered about the topic. Ask them what other specifics, details, expansions and explanations they would want and need if they were in the audience. If they were going to your presentation, what would they want to know?

This approach is particularly useful if it is the first time you are delivering certain content (e.g. if it is a one-off or first in a series) and/or if it is the first time you are delivering to a particular type of audience.

As a presenter, it is good to know that you are answering questions for the audience and 'ticking their boxes' so they will leave with something more than they came with. This is a key step in 'closing the gap'. If you know that your topic and content is going to be of interest to the audience and you have received external feedback to verify this, you are getting closer to the mind of the audience. You have already forged a connection and you are not even in the room with them!

Depending on the situation, another approach would be to contact members of the audience and invite questions before-hand. Then you can decide what is inside and outside the scope of your presentation. Alternatively, it may make you reconsider the scope of the presentation. When running corporate training courses, if we know a group want a particular slant to the training or a focus on a particular set of solutions, then we can see where this fits in and adapt that part of the course. Or if what the group wants is significantly different to the course material, we might recommend an alternative approach.

So how does checking with others help? It helps centre you on the needs of the audience, gives you information and makes you consider things you may not have thought of otherwise. In addition, it helps you predict questions, so you can prepare for what you might be asked and hence feel more confident.

A mismatch between the presenter's material and the audience's map of the world (including what the audience know, believe, have experienced, what's important to them and what are interested in) may increase the psychological gap between the presenter and audience. When there is a psychological gap, the audience may feel that the material doesn't relate to them and so they simply 'switch off'.

In addition, if a presenter does not check, they may know the topic well but make assumptions about other people's knowledge. There is an interesting piece of psychology in action here. When we learn something and we have known it for a while, we often assume other people know that information too (or at least the basics of it). It is as if it has become 'obvious'. The same is true for jargon; when we use a piece of jargon for long enough, we may assume others know it too. New knowledge and jargon eventually becomes the 'norm' in our map of the world and then we find ourselves surprised if others do not know it.

7) Arrangement of Content

Arranging the content means looking at the 'data' and deciding what content categories the data might fit into. What key content areas does the data suggest? What would fit into each category?

In order to break the topic into key areas, it helps some people to imagine they are working with a team of people (even if they are really going to present alone) and each person will be taking a section of the topic to present. If you were working with a team, how would you divide your presentation up? What distinct area would each person cover to avoid repeating what others had said?

In terms of categorising, consider how many key areas are sensible to have. This will partly depend on the time you have available and how complex or simple you want to make it. The more key areas, the more complex and unwieldy the whole thing becomes. We would recommend that each tier/level have no more than 5-7 key areas. If you are doing a short presentation (e.g. 15 minutes) then keep it down to about 3 key areas. If you have a short time period and too many key areas, you will find yourself rushing, overrunning and confusing people through overload. If your ten minute session is called: 'The Seven Keys to Effective Meetings', be prepared to skim through this session without much explanation!

If you have too many categories you may need to incorporate/amalgamate some of the areas together or reduce the scope of the presentation to fit the time available. You might then drop some of the content and give references and access to further information via a handout, website etc.

Once you have your key areas, each area will then break down into further detail, which brings us on to the next step...

8) Steps

The word 'Steps' carries an ambiguity here in representing 'tiers' of information/detail and also a process/sequence. Now we have our content and our categories, it is time to 'organise the data' by sorting the data in each category (into levels of detail) and then establishing an order.

In terms of the tiers, the levels will usually follow the pattern outlined below, starting with large chunk size (big picture) down into smaller chunk size (details):

Level	Tier	Questions	Example
1	Presentation Topic	What is the title of your presentation? What is it about?	*Effective Meetings*
2	Sub-Topics	Within the topic, what are the key areas that you will be covering?	1. *Preparing for meetings* 2. *Setting agendas* 3. *Chairing effectively* 4. *Dealing with difficulties*
3	Top level data	What key information will you be covering in each key area?	*1a. Why?* *1b. What?* *1c. Who?* *1d. Where?* *1e. When?*
4	Detail	What detail will you cover for the key information?	*1d i. Venue location* *1d ii. Room layout* *1d iii. Equipment*
5	Detailed details	What further details will you	*1d ii (a) Boardroom style* *1d ii (b) Theatre style*

		cover within each detail?	1d ii (c) Cabaret style 1d ii (d) U-Shape

The table above is an example of levels of detail, with the data getting more and more specific as you look down the table. Understanding the levels of detail can help you to stay at the appropriate level (and avoid getting bogged down in details and skipping too lightly over important points). The less the audience knows about a topic, the more detailed you may need to be if you want full understanding.

What if you find that some of the content data could be covered in more than one area of the presentation? By knowing that there are links in your presentation, you can decide where to cover it. You can then refer to it and that you will come back to it, or add more detail to it later. As long as you keep this to a minimum, you can create a sense of curiosity in the audience; it is as if you have 'opened a box' that you are going to explore and close later.

In terms of sequence, you will need to consider what seems to logically follow what? What needs to be explained before other things can be covered? What is reliant on what? Not only is a well sequenced presentation easier to remember, it is also easier to follow and learn from. By being easier to follow, it becomes more interesting and engaging and so the 'presenter-audience gap' decreases.

Methods of Organising, Categorising and Ordering the 'Steps'

A good method for categorising, chunking and sequencing will allow you to 'hang' your data around a structure and determine what level the pieces of data sit. You need to be able to differentiate between high level chunk size (e.g. 'Meetings') and low level (detailed) chunk size (e.g. 'One of the 3 golden rules for making an agenda engaging').

The radiant 'spider diagram' approach

Another approach to organising your content is the 'radiant thinking' approach, e.g. using 'spider diagrams' which give you a framework to break your presentation/training down into parts (key chunks, components). Write your topic title in the middle of the page with a circle round it. Then write the subtopics branching outwards from your main topic. The content data will then fit into the subtopics. You can then put the data into a logical order/sequence and sort for levels of detail.

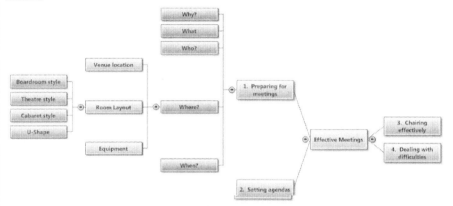

If necessary, you can then convert the data from the spider diagram into a linear format. For example, using the data from the table above:

Effective Meetings
 1. Preparing for meetings
    a. Why?
    b. What?
    c. Who?
    d. Where
        i. Venue location
        ii. Room layout
            1. Boardroom style
            2. Theatre style
            3. Cabaret style
            4. U-Shape
        iii. Equipment
    e. When?
 2. Setting agendas
 3. Chairing effectively
 4. Dealing with difficulties

In summary, the benefits of categorising, chunking and sequencing are that:

- You know where everything fits
- You have a logical process
- You are less likely to miss anything important
- You are more likely to remember the flow and the content

9) Take-Aways

Although we covered this to some extent at the start of the BROADCAST preparation, it is important to return to the question of what will the audience take away from the presentation/training? What will the session give them? What are the benefits to the audience of attending your session and listening to/learning the content?

In addition to thinking about what the audience will get by attending, you will also want to consider: What do you want the audience to know *and* do as a result of the presentation? If a presentation (and particularly training) doesn't result in any change of behaviour, what was the point? Behaviour change may come as a result of a change in knowledge, skill and/or attitude, so which of these areas are you seeking to address?

In summary, before delivering any presentation or training, ask yourself: What will the audience gain by (a) attending and listening to the content and (b) taking action after the presentation, i.e. doing what you want them to do.

Physical Take-aways: Handouts and Visual Aids

Once you have organised, categorised and ordered your content, you have, in effect, structured any handouts (e.g. notes and workbooks/manuals) and/or visual aids (e.g. power-point slides) you are going to use, assuming you are using them. This way, the logic and flow of your handouts/visuals are the same as your presentation/training, which avoids too much dancing back and forth between pages and/or slides.

The first slide or page is likely to be an overview of what you are going to be covering. This information comes from the top level of your 'spider diagram', i.e. the key categories/headings of your content. Then the following slides/pages will reflect the next levels of detail/information from the diagram. The amount of slides/pages will be dependent on the level of detail you are covering which in turn should be informed by the amount of time you have.

If you are designing workbooks, consider how much information you are giving. Are you writing them a book type manual or sets of steps and bullet point tips? Or are you going for the 'question with empty box' approach which allows people to fill in information for themselves as they go through the course? Or perhaps you want a mixture of the above? If in doubt, look at some other trainers' workbooks and manuals to find the model that works best for you.

Model Making

As a model presenter:
- Get clear about the aim and purpose of the presentation/ training
- Prepare well enough to have a memorable and logical structure
- Decide what content is in the scope of your presentation/ training

The Model Presenter

Chapter 5

Structure: Preparing to Deliver a Presentation

In This Chapter...

In this chapter, we will be exploring some of the best practice around delivering a presentation and you will discover a couple of surprisingly simple changes you can make to the traditional approach which will strengthen your presentations immensely.

We will be exploring the following questions:

- What is the most effective structure for a presentation?
- How do you make a positive impression with your introduction and conclusion (and why is it important to do so)?
- How do you make sure your main points are flexible enough to be shortened or extended during a presentation?

The Presentation Overview

Consider the flow of a traditional presentation... an introduction followed by the main points and then a summary followed by questions:

Introduction > Main Points/Content > Summary/Conclusion > Questions

The Model Presenter

Imagine the scene: the presenter is coming to the conclusion of a very well delivered presentation. The introduction has engaged the audience, the content has been concise and informative, the summary has pulled it all together and the ending is strong. Now the speaker asks if there are any questions. Soon the questions dry up and there is silence in the room. Where does the speaker go then? At best, they thank the audience; at worst we hear those three all-too-common words... "That's it really"!

The problem with the traditional format is that if there are no questions at the end, there is a possible 'tumble-weed' moment as the speaker waits for someone to say something. Then, if there *are* questions at the end, the power of the final message of the presenter is potentially lost.

In addition, if the summary is powerful, people may be put off asking questions. If the presentation seems to be 'closed' by the summary, there is no psychological space for questions. If there are questions, we go back into the content of the presentation, perhaps specific details or 'sideways' questions that take us into other areas. Having concluded, the presenter is still left with the need to deal with the 'random-land' of questions at the end.

The final part of the presentation is what the audience is left with and hence the success of the presentation becomes reliant on the audience asking sensible, supportive questions that the presenter can answer easily and effectively! It is not surprising that some presenters get anxious when the outcome of their presentation is reliant on other people.

If we want the audience to feel inspired and perhaps motivated to action, having questions at the end is a huge risk, since our final message is likely to be diluted, lost, countered or forgotten. So here is the simplest change for the most impressive results:

Put the summary at the end, after the question session!

By ending with your summary, you finish how you want to, completely within your control. You take the audience where you want them to go. You contain the questions and close them down. You might even refer to some of the questions on your summary. You leave them with the message and emotion that you *want* to leave them with. You can finish on a high note, on a serious note, or with a laugh. Your choice!

Introduction > Main Points/Content > Questions > Summary/Conclusion

In terms of how much time you might spend on each section, a very rough guideline would be:

Introduction	5%-15%
Main Points/Content	60%-70%
Questions	10%-20%
Summary/Conclusion	5%-10%

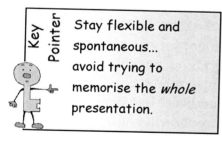

Key Pointer

Stay flexible and spontaneous... avoid trying to memorise the *whole* presentation.

As a recommendation, avoid trying to memorise the whole presentation word for word (unless you are one of those people with an extraordinary memory). The problem with 'scripting' is that it can come across as overly rehearsed and lacking in spontaneity (and hence personality). In addition, if something knocks you off script, it can be challenging to get back on it. So have a few 'run-throughs' to get a sense of the timing, but give yourself space for flexibility.

If you are going to memorise any part of the presentation, make it the introduction (and possibly the summary). The introduction will be brief and is the time to make an impact through being professional and clear. Rehearsing the introduction allows you use more compelling language that you wouldn't normally use when talking on autopilot. Be careful to maintain your personality in the delivery however.

Opening your Presentation: The Introduction

Your introduction is quite possibly the most important part of your presentation because it will determine whether the people in the audience are going to listen and get engaged with what you have to say. This is your only opportunity to make a good first impression. In the first few moments, the audience will be sorting you and your presentation into a category of 'worth listening to' or 'not worth listening to'. Once you are in one category or the other, it will take something significant to shift categories. The introduction is your moment to build connection and credibility with the audience. When you have these things, you will tend to be more persuasive and influential than if you do not.

On the note of credibility, we have noticed that some presenters seem to want to put themselves down at the start, saying things like: "I'll try not to send you to sleep" or "I'm not very good with the IT stuff" or "I'll try and cover this as quickly as possible as it's not particularly riveting". Perhaps a presenter might put themselves down to manage the expectations of the audience but unless you are doing this for some other purpose, it probably will not win you any credibility points. If you know that you do this yourself, consider the positive intention (i.e. the positive benefits you might get) of being self-critical and find another, more credible way of meeting this positive intention.

As a rule of thumb, you would tend to write your introduction after you have worked out the details of your main points. This means that you then know *what* you are introducing! The length of your introduction would normally be about 5%-15% of your allocated

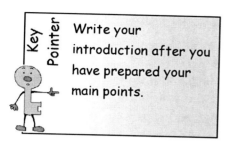

Key Pointer: Write your introduction after you have prepared your main points.

presentation time. If you have 10 minutes you would usually want to keep your introduction down to about a minute.

There are seven key pieces of information that you should aim to get into your introduction. Although the order below provides a good starting point, the items are flexible and some of them can be mixed up and/or combined.

1. Attention grabber
2. Subject/main message
3. What's in it for them?
4. Who us, who me and why me?
5. Timings
6. Headlines
7. Ground-rules

1. Attention grabber

It is vital that you open your presentation in a way that will capture the attention of your audience. Whatever device you choose, make sure it is relevant, sensible and appropriate. The attention grabber has a 'risk factor' associated with it which could make or break the credibility of the presenter and/or presentation. What do you feel comfortable doing or saying that is memorable for the right reasons? For example, some presenters might use humour as an attention grabber. The risk is that this could be excruciating if it doesn't get a laugh (known as the 'tumbleweed' moment). Humour is a strange one! Our recommendation is to use humour as an attention grabber either when it is spontaneous or when you are absolutely certain and congruent that what you are going to say is funny to a large percentage of the population! An embarrassed audience is probably not what you want for starters unless you are purposely causing embarrassment and awkwardness to make a specific point.

Some attention grabbers have a low risk factor and others are higher depending on the context. With each of the following, you would usually want to avoid clichés (i.e. what everyone else says/does) and obscure references (i.e. what no-one else says/does!)

Here are a few examples of attention grabbers:

- Tell a story: Keep it very short!
- Refer to the occasion or the venue.
- Offer a sincere compliment.
- Start with a quotation: Avoid being too pretentious!
- Make a significant statement: Something to get people thinking, for example "There is no such thing as failure..."
- Use a statistic.
- Make a promise: A friend of ours used to start courses with the line: "Hi, my name's Richard and the answer to your question is '4.30'" (which was the finishing time).
- Ask a challenging question: Get people thinking, for example: "When was the last time you told one your manager that they are doing a great job?"
- Use a dramatic visual or sound: Make sure it is relevant and linked to what you are presenting rather than some random sound.

If you follow a speaker who engaged positively with the audience, make a complimentary link to them or what they said. This may allow you to "steal" rapport.

If you use a powerful attention grabber, pause for a moment afterwards to let the audience get it. Some presenters make a profound statement but then reduce its impact by carrying on talking as if it wasn't significant. Whilst not a long uncomfortable pause (unless that is part of the attention grabber itself), it needs to be long enough for the audience to process what you have said/done and perhaps why you have said/done it.

2. Subject/main message

In your introduction, this part may just be a few words, i.e. the title of your presentation. Although a brief few words, it can help to make sure everyone is in the right room!

3. What's in it for them?

In chapter 4, using the BROADCAST model, you will have determined the benefits to the audience of attending, listening and engaging with your presentation. This is the time to let them know.

4. Who us, who me and why me?

If you are representing an organisation/department/group then start with the 'us' part and let the audience know who you represent. Then let the audience know who you are (particularly your name) and why it is you delivering the presentation. Give them a sense of your experience and how you are qualified to be there. This is your opportunity to introduce your credentials and build your credibility. A few sentences will usually make the point since you walk a fine line between under-doing it and overdoing it.

As an aside, many people start an introduction with their name. Whilst there is nothing wrong with this (and indeed may prove to be a safe bet) it could be deemed a little 'too safe'. Your name is not much of an attention grabber to people who don't know you (unless you happen to share your name with a celebrity). Johnny Cash was one of those rare people who could walk onto the stage and say: "Hello, I'm Johnny Cash" and the audience would go wild. Most of us don't have that level of impact by name alone, though it is an interesting goal!

5. Timings

Although the audience may already know, it is worth reminding them how long you will be talking for. Even when people are looking forward to hearing you, they still like to know when things will be wrapping up!

6. Headlines

The headlines section is an overview of what you are going to be covering in your presentation. At this stage you will tell the audience the key areas that you will be covering. Unless you have a long period of time, i.e. hours rather than minutes, you are best off giving the 'subtitles' at this point rather than any further detail. The trick here is not to get into the content no matter how tempting. All you are doing is putting up signs as to where you are going through your presentation.

7. Ground-rules

Ground rules allow you to set expectations and to put in contingencies which in turn will help you to control the group and prevent certain issues (e.g. switch phones off). If necessary, this would also be the time to let people know of any other logistics (e.g. when the break is, where to get coffee, where the toilets are).

The classic ground rule is about 'questions' and this is also useful for the audience. Let the audience know *when* you want questions, i.e. throughout, at the end or both. The general guideline here is if you are confident with your material, take questions throughout. If the topic is contentious, complex or new to you, you might ask for questions at the end. Of course, you might give time for questions at the end of each segment.

An Example Introduction: Exploring Dreams

"The average person will spend almost 10 years of their life dreaming and yet most people are oblivious to this intriguing twilight realm. Welcome to the dream world! My name is Joe and I have been researching sleep and dreams for the last twenty-five years. Over the next hour, we will be decoding dreams and exploring if dreams have meaning. You will discover some of the science behind dream research and also learn a technique to help you take control of your dreams. If you have any questions, ask them as we go and then I'll also leave a few minutes at the end too."

Main Points

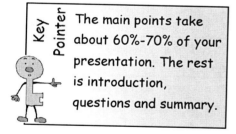

The main points take about 60%-70% of your presentation. The rest is introduction, questions and summary.

The main part of your presentation will be the content/information that you want to share with the audience, i.e. that which you prepared in the previous chapter. Time-wise, the main points in total will usually take up about 60%-70% of your presentation. So in a ten minute presentation you would spend about six and a half minutes on the main points.

As discussed in chapter 4, depending on how long you have, it is perhaps wise to keep the number of key areas down to a realistic minimum. For each key area of the presentation, you may want to prioritise and hence organise your data to distinguish between what you really need to get across from the non-essentials. In order to prioritise, you might use something like the NIC System (Need-Intend-Could) to control what you want to say...

The Model Presenter

The NIC System

Have you ever seen a presenter run out of time or spend too long on seemingly irrelevant material? Have you ever known a presenter to waffle?

When we prepare a presentation, we will have a list of content. Some of the content will be more crucial and/or pressing than other parts. Some of the content might be 'nice to have' or 'interesting filler', whereas some of it may be 'essential to convey'. So, when you are preparing your presentation, look at your content and ask yourself: "Which parts stand out as more important than the others?"

To help you prioritise your content, consider the NIC system:

The NIC System

Need	This is the information you need to get across to the audience, i.e. the key messages.
Intend	This is the information it would be good to share if there is time. This might be more detailed data and/or key examples.
Could	This is the information that backs up what you are saying. It is usually more detailed or 'sideways' information and examples/anecdotes that might come out in the questions phase or that you could use if there are no questions and you have time to spare. Might be additional information you would share in a handout.

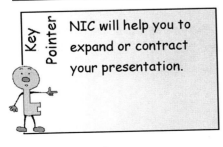

Key Pointer

NIC will help you to expand or contract your presentation.

The NIC System helps you to prioritise and focus on the most important points and core messages. You might imagine this as three layered circles with 'need' in the middle, then 'intend', then the outside circle being 'could'. It is important to sort the layers out in your mind so you know what level of information you are at when you are presenting. Some people colour code the information in their notes giving them an option to go more detailed or stay at the core 'need' level.

One of the most useful aspects of the NIC system is that it allows you to manage your time more effectively during a presentation. One of the key skills of a presenter is the ability to manage the time available. It is the poor presenter that overruns since it shows a disregard and disrespect for other people, both the audience and other speakers. By having prioritised your information, you can 'concertina' your presentation to expand it or contract it as necessary. Sometimes you may find that you have less time than you expected because a previous speaker has overrun. At this point you can begin to drop some of your 'could' and 'intend' and focus on the 'need'. In addition, if you realise that you are running behind schedule yourself (perhaps through adding in extra information or handling questions throughout) you can cut the latter sections of the presentation down to the 'need'.

Time can play tricks on a presenter. Sometimes it seems that you have run out of things to say and there is still plenty of time left. At other times, it feels like you have just drawn breath in to speak and your allocated time is almost up. The NIC system at least gives you flexibility to work with time seeming to speed up or slow down.

As a final point of time management and the NIC system: it is worth doing a run through of your presentation before the event with just the core 'need' material to see how long that takes. Bear in mind as well, that some presenters speed up when they are nervous and so they get through the material quicker on the day than they do in the run through.

Questions

The whole area of handling questions is dealt with in more detail in Chapter 10. However, in a presentation, you would probably want to use about 10%-20% of your time handling questions. This would be true if you are taking questions throughout the presentation or holding them for the end. Remember, the important thing here is to let the audience know in your introduction as to what you want them to do with their questions.

If you are handling questions before summarising (which we recommend), it is worth signposting to the audience that this is your intention. You might say: "Before I summarise and we wrap up, are there any questions?"If there are questions, handle them until the group are done (or you are running out of time). Then you might say something like: "Any more questions? No, okay, in summary..." If you are running out of time, you will need to let people know how you will answer their questions outside of the presentation.

Closing your Presentation: The Summary

The purpose of the summary/conclusion is to give a final overview and integrate the content of the presentation. It is *not* the time to introduce new data (unless you have a very specific reason, e.g. a teaser for what is coming later). You are bringing it all together... drawing to a close. You are reminding the audience of the key messages and the things you want them to take away and/or do. A nice way of completing is to reference back to your attention grabber at the start of the presentation, hence closing the loop and creating a neat and tidy package.

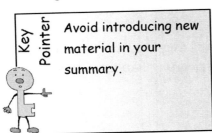

Key Pointer

Avoid introducing new material in your summary.

The summary section will tend to take about 5%-10% of the presentation, so keep it brief and snappy. The closing is perhaps equally important to the introduction: it needs to be clear and defined leaving the audience feeling motivated to act in a particular way. Your presentation needs to be delivered with this in mind. Make sure you have tied everything up.

Although you don't need to use all of the items below, here are a few things you might use in your closing:

- Remind the audience of the headlines (the areas you covered without going into the details).
- Summarise and recap the key messages.
- Next steps
- End like the beginning, i.e. refer back to your attention grabber in the introduction (the occasion, venue, statistic, question, anecdote/story, dramatic visual or sound).
- Final message
- Thank you

Although it may seem obvious, saying "thank you" at the end makes it clear to the audience that you have finished. Most audiences like the clarity of knowing that you are definitely complete, so make it easy for them.

An Example Conclusion: Exploring Dreams

"So tonight we have explored how to discover the meaning of dreams and we've looked at some of the science behind dream research. You've also now got a tool for exploring dreams from the inside. Dreams are an integral part of who we are... part of the human experience. It is up to you how fascinated you get about your unconscious mind and the messages it gives you. Start a dream diary and get familiar with how your dreaming mind works. Get engaged with that sleepy ten percent of your life! I don't know what

---

dreams you will dream when you sleep tonight, but may they be full of fascination. Thank you for coming and making tonight... a dream! Thank you."

Model Making

As a model presenter:
- Summarise the presentation after handling questions
- Keep your introduction and summary concise and compelling
- Prioritise your messages, from 'need' to get across through to 'could' say

Chapter 6

Designing and Delivering Training Courses

In This Chapter...

In this chapter, you will be discovering some different training and learning styles which will set a context for the IMPACT Formula for designing and delivering training sessions.

We will be exploring the following questions:

- What are some different training approaches?
- What are some of the different ways people learn and how do you accommodate those differences?
- What is the IMPACT Formula for designing and delivering training sessions?
- What are some different types of learning activities you can get a group doing?

Training Style and Approach

In chapter 3 we discussed approaches linked to 'pulling' and 'pushing' in order to engage the audience. It is worth revisiting that idea here in terms of training style. The most effective trainers use a contextual/situational approach, i.e. their style will be based on the experience and needs of the group. Using the 'push – pull' continuum, here are some different training styles for different situations:

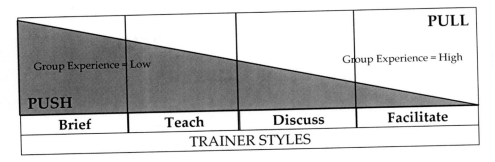

Brief
- Tell, inform.
- Focus on 'why' and 'what'.
- Useful for beginners (who are in a state of 'unconscious incompetence').

Teach
- Hands on, showing, imparting expertise. Taking/ answering questions and asking specific questions to test people's knowledge of what they are learning.
- Focus on 'how'.
- Useful for developing learners (who are in a state of 'conscious incompetence').

Discuss
- Consulting, hands off, coaching, supporting, involving and getting input from group, asking questions to help learners answer their own questions, overcome their own obstacles and solve their own problems.
- Focus on 'what if'.
- Useful for learners with experience (who are in a state of 'conscious competence').

Facilitate
- Aiding learner in going further, providing an environment for 'self-learning', asking self-

directed learning questions.
- Focus on 'who' and 'what do you need'
- Useful for more advanced learners (who are in a state of 'unconscious competence').

Matching Different Learning Styles

A Case In Point

Years ago, I remember a group of delegates where everyone sat quietly through the first part of the course. I began to 'up my game' and endeavoured to become as engaging as possible. The group got quieter instead of livelier. It wasn't until I 'gave up' and sat down that the group were more open to discussing the topics at hand. All was going well until I sent them off to do an activity. In the debrief it was apparent that they didn't actually do the activity, they just sat around and talked about it. They enjoyed the discussion and were very happy with the outcome. They said they learnt lots from hearing about other people's perspectives and experiences.

Although the scenario above was not completely unusual, we have experienced other groups that were impatient to get on and give it a go. They *wanted* to do something and any discussion was considered a hindrance.

Most groups have a mix of people with different preferences for how they want to learn. Understanding peoples' 'learning styles' will give you clues as to how to design training courses and also how to deliver them. A trainer who does not regard other peoples' learning styles will tend to teach from their own preference. This will work with some of the audience but is unlikely to appeal to everyone. The aim here is to develop flexibility.

You, yourself will have preferred methods of learning. Consider for a moment three or four things that you have learnt in the last year.

The Model Presenter

It might be from work, at home, linked to a hobby or from somewhere else where you have learnt something new. For each thing you learnt, ask yourself why you learnt it and how you learnt it (e.g. read a book, went on a course, browsed the internet, experimented, got some advice or coaching). Be as specific as you can be in terms of *what helped* you to learn it. Given all of your answers, what patterns can you see? What generalisations might you begin to make about your own learning preferences and style? And how does that reflect your preferred style of teaching and training?

Here we will be utilising two models which were both adapted from the works of David Kolb[1]. The first model is Honey and Mumford's[2] 'Learning Styles' (which is useful for identifying different types of learners) and Bernice McCarthy's[3] 4Mat system (which is useful in terms of designing training).

<u>1) Learning Styles</u>

From Kolb's material, Peter Honey and Alan Mumford identified four 'learning styles' that people have when they are learning new things. Although we *can* learn in different ways, most of us have ways that we *prefer* to learn.

As a trainer, it is helpful to know that there are different preferences and styles of learning. If we were unaware of individual differences we would likely 'teach' people in our own personal style (or in a traditional 'how we were taught to teach' manner). Whilst teaching approaches may have changed in schools now, my (Joe's) general experience was that teachers would talk and write on a board whilst we had to shut up and write things down (known as the 'talk and chalk' approach). Of course, this worked for some of the kids in the classroom, but it didn't really engage me. My mind would quickly wander to dungeons and dragons and magic and monsters... sadly we didn't have lessons in such things!

The four learning styles are: *activist, reflector, theorist* and *pragmatist*. In essence:

- the *activist* prefers to learn through doing things, through being in the driving seat as it were, at the centre of the experience,
- the *reflector* prefers to stand back, observe and ask questions from different angles,
- the *theorist* prefers to understand the background, model or concept behind the learning... a framework to hang the learning on,
- the *pragmatist* prefers to know the steps and to learn through a process of experimentation, tried and tested or otherwise.

Here are some generic approaches we have found for appealing to each learning style:

Activist
- Action. Give them something 'hands on' to do and experience.
- Skills practice, role play.
- Problem solving activities.

Reflector
- Case studies.
- Discussion groups.
- Brainstorming ideas.

Theorist
- Background theory.
- Showing and creating models.
- Sorting and putting things into categories.

Pragmatist
- Practical problem situations to resolve.
- Coming up with best practice.
- Action planning.

There is a general flow to training, whether you are working one-to-one or with groups. The process picks up each learning style along the way and runs in a cycle:

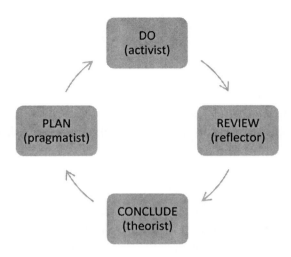

The question is: where do you start? We have found that if you are working 'free-flow' with a group, after setting a context you can start anywhere and then go round the cycle (see below). For example, you might introduce a topic and then start with a model, show them the steps, give them a go and then review it after. Or you might give people a chance to try something out, followed by reviewing, concluding and then action plans for next time.

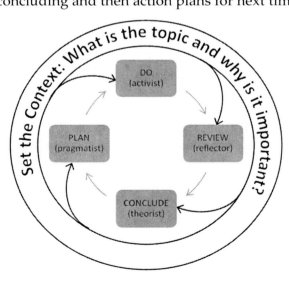

If you are working one to one with someone, use their learning style as the starting point. To establish their preference quickly and practically, you can ask them: "Where would you like to start? Do you want to have a go… or I can show you or give you a bit about the background or give you the key steps?" If they have a preference they will tell you and you can start there… and then go through the rest of the steps. For example, if they are more of a reflector, show them, then draw some key points out then give them the steps and then let them have a go. A pragmatist might prefer to start with knowing the steps and then have a go followed by a bit of practical reflection and discussion.

2) The 4Mat System

Bernice McCarthy developed the 4Mat system as a way of modelling an effective teaching session. The 4Mat draws from Kolb and provides a systematic approach using the four steps: Why? What? How? What if?

The system works around the idea that, first things first, people need to know why they are doing something. Then we can tell them what they are doing, including the model or relevant background. They are then ready to find out how to do it and then give it a go. After they have given it a go, there is time for reflection.

To give you a little more detail, these are the kind of things that might be included in each section:

1) Why	Once you have stated what the topic is, you need to give the audience a reason to be interested and engaged with the topic. This is particularly important in a learning environment and can be done by giving some of the following: • Context: What is the bigger picture in which this topic sits? What are some of the key issues, mistakes and problems with the current situation?

	• Purpose: Why is this topic important? • Benefits: How will knowing/learning about this help the audience? What will they gain? What will it give them?
2) What?	This is where you introduce the concept, theory and/or model. What are they here to learn?
3) How?	To make sure there is something practical and applicable in the learning, the audience will want to know what to do with it and how to apply it. Outline the steps, procedure or process. Make sure the steps are logical and clear. Then get the audience doing something with it... give them some active practice.
4) What if?	After they have had a go, you can debrief what they experienced. How did they find it? What happened? What did they discover/learn? Then you can take the learning wider to further applications in the 'real world'. Where could they apply it and how? What might be challenging ('what if...') and how might that be handled.

Learning Styles vs 4MAT

As you may have already established, there is a common pattern with Honey and Mumford's Learning Styles and McCarthy's 4Mat. Aside from them both using Kolb as a platform, they map together well enough:

Stage	**1**	**2**	**3**	**4**
4MAT	Why	What	How	What if
Equivalent Learning style	Context set is useful for all working styles	Theorist	Pragmatist (process/steps) & Activist (action/doing)	Reflector

The difference is that 4Mat is a system that always follows the same sequence whereas a learning styles approach may start anywhere (but still needs an overall 'why' to start with).

Learning Inductively vs Deductively

Whilst it is our experience that most people *do* like to know why they are doing something, if the trainer is trustworthy and credible in the eyes of the group, people are usually happy to do something if they know that the 'why' will emerge from experimentation. This is an example of deductive versus inductive learning.

Deductive learning means taking a theory or model and then applying it to create our own examples and experience. Inductive learning means having our own experiences and examples and then creating a theory or model from this.

Most professional training will be deductive, where participants are provided with information and then given an opportunity to apply it to their working environment. Inductive training works particularly well with personal development courses where participants draw from their own experiences to reflect and draw conclusions. However, even with inductive training, in order to get to the 'why' through doing something first, there still needs to be an overview of *how* they are to do the exercise and a 'process why' (i.e. the reason you are doing it this way round, e.g. "I'm going to throw you straight into the next activity so that you can determine the purpose of what you discovered afterwards.")

4MAT would be considered a deductive approach to teaching where the model is set out first and then the participants get to apply this for themselves (with some possible inductive learning at the end in the 'what if' reflective stage).

The IMPACT Formula: A Practical Method for Designing & Delivering Training

To bring this 'learning styles' piece to a practical conclusion, there is a formula that we have developed for designing and delivering training courses which we call IMPACT. Not only is this a formula for the overall course itself, it also works for each session/subtopic within the course. The example below, 'Delegation', might be a subtopic in a 'Managing people' course (in which the IMPACT formula would be repeated for each subtopic, e.g. 'Motivation', 'Coaching', 'Feedback' and 'Dealing with Difficult People'):

IMPACT	Trainer Action	Example	Learning Style
Introduction	State the topic for the session and set the scene/context. Why is this important? Benefits to them in being effective. Get some previous experiences from the group on this topic.	*"So now we move to 'Delegation'... an essential skill that some managers get right but some get very wrong! Talk to the person sitting next to you for a couple of minutes and come up with some things that work and some that don't work with delegation."*	All Why?
Model	Introduce the model, theory, 'quadrant', best practice, key skills needed. Give examples.	*"Here are the four keys to delegating effectively... 1...2...3...4"*	Theorist What?
Process	Introduce the key steps/ stages or phases.	*"And so the steps to delegating effectively are..."*	Pragmatist How?
Action	Get the group doing an activity/exercise. Let them try it out and give feedback as necessary.	*"Think of a task you might delegate to a person you manage and go through the steps with a partner."*	Activist How?
Challenges	Explore difficulties, barriers, obstacles and problems. Then	*"What might get in the way to you delegating back at work?... Now how might*	Reflector Theorist

	explore solutions	*you prevent or cure each of those?"*	
			What if?
Test	Explore applications. Where might they put this topic into practice in their real world? How will they do it? Action plan.	*"Think about the workplace now and write down some situations where you could apply this. Plan how you will do this."*	Pragmatist Activist
			What if?

Notes on the IMPACT Formula

a) Introduction

At the start of a training course, the first part of the introduction phase would include:

- Welcome
- Course topic
- Who are we (e.g. company or department), who am I and why am I the trainer? (This is an opportunity to build connection and credibility.)
- Who are you? (Course participants say who they are, where from etc.)
- Course objectives and overview of course content
- Participant aims for the course
  - o What would you like to achieve as a result of being on the course?
  - o How will you know you have achieved it?
  - o How will others know?
- Domestics (where things are, timings, breaks, lunch) and ground-rules (guidelines and boundaries e.g. confidentiality, phones & laptops off etc.)

After the course/personal introductions and aims have been covered, you would then move on to the context setting for the course topic (e.g. 'Project Management') or for a particular sub-topic within the course (e.g. 'planning').

After a few words about the subject, e.g. what is 'X' & why is it important/valuable/useful, it can be helpful to get the group identifying what works and what does not work in the context of the topic. They might explore best practice and common issues and concerns that they have with the subject (e.g. through 'plenary' discussion or getting them into subgroups). It is important to keep a bit of variety in this phase, so here are a few different ways of asking for the information:

- What are some examples of good/poor X?
- What is best practice with X and what could go wrong with X? What are some top tips and key mistakes made with X?
- Why does X succeed or fail? Why does X work/not always work?
- What are the advantages/disadvantages of X?
- What happens when X is done well or poorly? Benefits vs consequences?

This kind of exercise/discussion is useful because it:

- Elicits group & individual 'pet theories'.
- Acts cathartically as a 'therapeutic' session for the group, talking through issues in a contained way.
- 'Pulls' issues out of the group early on so they are less likely to go on about it later.
- Gives a contained time and space for 'naysayers' and 'negative thinkers'.
- Allows the group to start a 'turnaround' process in getting to list out some desired outcomes, learning points and/or solutions.

b) Action phase

During the Action phase, when getting the group to do things, there are a range of activities you can use. When designing a course, in order to keep the group engaged, make sure there are different types of exercises[4], for example:

Activity	Advantage/ When to use	Disadvantage/ Issues	Tips
Case studies	Allows exploration of a situation from a detached perspective (what could X do?) or associated (what would you do?)	There will never be enough information for some people and too much for others!	Make sure they are relevant to the group.
Skills practice	Allows people to give it a go, to practice and test out the topic and concepts in a safe environment.	Some people get nervous about practising something new, particularly if it is in front of others.	Where possible let people do skills practices in the 'privacy' of pairs/ trios rather than in front of the audience. Keep an eye/ear on everyone.
Role plays	Allows people to try out new behaviours in a low risk environment.	Many people dislike 'role play' on principle and say it is 'unrealistic'.	If people don't like 'role plays,' call them 'interactive case studies'!

Experience sharing	Provides an opportunity for people to share ideas, experiences and concerns. This can help to normalise experiences – "I'm not the only one!"	Some may dominate the conversation. If the group has had a collective negative experience, they could go into a downward spiral or 'shark frenzy'.	Contain it. Have them write the bullet points of their experiences on a flip chart. This helps to disassociate any issues and keep the focus on the task you set.
Problem solving	Gives a variety of activities, from designing and 'building things' to more theoretical numerical, lateral or puzzle solving.	Can cause frustration if the problem is too hard for the group, or presented at the wrong time or doesn't match the mood of the group. People start questioning the exercise.	Be ready to give hints or clues. Normalise the fact that 'most groups' don't get it immediately. Be prepared to debrief the exercise if no-one gets the answer.
Quiz	Can test knowledge or get people looking through a document seeking answers to questions (e.g. HR policy).	If the questions are too challenging or ambiguous, some people give up. Alternatively, if it is too easy, people may feel patronised.	Put yourself in the shoes of the first time learner. How would you answer these questions? Also, test the questions out with colleagues beforehand.
Creativity	Allows groups to generate ideas or design something, e.g. through brainstorming.	Some people seem to get cynical about the concept of 'brainstorming' (the same people that don't like 'management speak' and jargon).	Small subgroups, no more than 5 or 6. Set clear outcomes and give guidelines for how the group should work together.

Contingency planning	Allows a group to explore what could go wrong/ what is the problem with a topic or project and then come up with solutions and ideas	Unchecked, a group may get into tiny details of problems or start coming up with highly unlikely scenarios, e.g. what could go wrong with meetings? 'Invasion by aliens'.	Give the group structure and perhaps an idea of how many examples they should be aiming for.
Icebreakers and 'energisers'	Can be helpful as a 'get to know you' exercise. Can raise the energy of a group, e.g. after lunchtime.	May be seen as time wasting, particularly if there is no significant learning point. Can be seen as 'old hat' by those who have been on many courses and have to through a ball around for the fifteenth time! Can be perceived as childish.	Keep them brief, relevant to the topic and appropriate to the mood and level of the group.

Activities can carry a 'risk factor' when not designed or implemented effectively. As a general rule, make sure all activities you run are:

- *Relevant to the group*: If people can't find any relevance to their own experience, they tend to start criticising the activity.
- *Purposeful*: Make sure that activities are not just there to 'kill time' (or are open to being perceived that way).
- *Time appropriate*: Consider a time/learning ratio where the time spent on an activity needs to equate to the value the group will get out of it.

The Model Presenter

- *Well managed*: Be aware of the potential for people to fall out with one another or for conflict to arise, particularly when people know one another already.
- *Minimise the risk of 'failure'*: Some problems may be too difficult to solve (e.g. within a particular timeframe). How will you handle any frustration? What will you do if the group cannot come to an answer?
- *Well briefed and debriefed*: Make sure the activities are well explained and clear. Provide written instructions if necessary. Then after the activity, ensure it is given meaning and applied back to the group's real world.

Model Making

As a model presenter:
- Adapt your approach to suit the needs, experience and learning styles of the audience
- Give people a range of relevant learning activities to keep their interest
- Use the IMPACT formula to design and deliver your training sessions

Chapter 7

Body, Voice and Emotion

In This Chapter...

In this chapter, you will gain some insights into the concept of 'purposeful' body and voice in order to deliver your message more professionally. You will be given some tips on managing emotions and reminded of the difference between effective and ineffective use of body and voice.

We will be exploring the following questions:

- How can you use your voice and body language to congruently deliver your message?
- How can you be more purposeful with your body language and voice?
- What are some ways of getting the audience's attention back to you?
- What is the body-voice-emotion connection?
- How can you manage other people's emotions?

Modelling Body, Voice and Emotion

Given that the subject of this book is presenting and training, the goal of the next two chapters is to help you become more purposeful with your body language, your voice tone and your language. By raising your awareness of how you act and speak, you will become more engaging in your style.

The Model Presenter

Body language and voice convey how you feel and can help you to manage your emotions. Imagine becoming more purposeful with your emotions when in front of an audience, shifting elegantly from one chosen state to another. As you experience resourceful emotions, your audience is likely to follow. If *you* experience and portray confidence, then your audience is more likely to feel confident (in you and in your material).

Key Pointer

Raise your self-awareness...
Record yourself!

We recommend initially that you observe and adapt your body language and voice *outside* of the presentation environment. Notice yourself in meetings and conversations when you are not really the centre of attention. Record yourself delivering presentations (either audio or video) and listen/watch back at a reflective time. The first step in making changes to ingrained habits is to realise that you have them. Then choose to play with and make changes when the 'risk' is low. When you are presenting/training, however, *focus on delivering your message*... let the body language and voice sort itself out! Of course, if you notice you are doing something unhelpful and can make the change easily there and then, do it. The point here is that delivering a message to an audience can be challenging enough without having to focus on normally unconscious behaviours too.

Congruence

A Case In Point

A speaker stands awkwardly in front of the audience, shifting backwards and forwards on his feet. He tells the customer that they should be confident in the new product line. Although he says all the right words, his eyes focus on the floor and his voice drops off at the end of each sentence. How confident do you imagine the customer will feel?

Congruence is about alignment. When you are congruent you will be delivering a consistent message throughout your body, voice and words. Everything lines up... your posture will match your gestures, tonality, language and expressions etc.

There is an unfortunate myth based on research done in the 1960s by a man called Albert Mehrabian[1] that body language equals 55% of our communication, voice equals 38% and words equal 7%. In his book *Silent Messages*, Mehrabian contextualised this percentage to a very specific phenomenon, i.e. how we perceive incongruence. It was never meant to relate to overall communication, but the myth has perpetuated through trainers, books and media.

If there is incongruence between non-verbal and verbal communication, the audience will tend to get mixed messages and they may feel a sense (albeit small) of distrust or confusion. Incongruence is often a form of unconscious 'leakage', where some part of the system communicates a contradictory message. Such incongruence can indicate an internal conflict in the speaker or a conscious desire to mislead the audience.

Imagine a speaker starting with the words: "It's lovely to be here with you today". If this was delivered with a downbeat, bored sounding voice, then the voice does not match the words. Too much incongruence between the voice, words and/or body language will tend to reduce the speaker's credibility. For this reason, we encourage you to develop your congruence. Find ways to believe in yourself and your message and then this will be reflected in the audience.

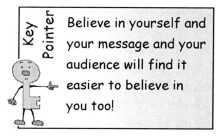

Key Pointer

Believe in yourself and your message and your audience will find it easier to believe in you too!

The following sections on body language and voice are a starting point, giving you some ideas on what to look out for if you choose to observe yourself. Alternatively, they may be areas to get feedback on from supportive friends and colleagues.

We have used the idea of effective and ineffective body language and voice. This is meant to be from the audience perspective and reflects what we have observed over the years. However, there may be odd moments here and there where you might choose to use some of the less effective behaviour for a reason. Our overall aim is to encourage you to be <u>purposeful</u> in what you do with your physiology, voice, emotion and language.

<u>Purposeful Body Language</u>

Body language includes all of our physiological behaviours:

- *Posture*: How do you hold yourself? E.g. slumped or shoulders back?
- *Stance*: How do you stand? E.g. one foot forward or both together, facing the audience directly or slightly away?
- *Gestures*: What do you do with your hands?
- *Movement*: How much of your body moves? At what pace?
- *Facial expressions*: What emotions do you convey with your expressions? What do you do with your facial muscles, your mouth, your eyes, your forehead, your chin etc.?
- *Eye contact*: Where do you look? To the audience? To the back of the room? How many people do you make eye contact with? For how long?

It is perhaps tempting to want to 'read' someone's body language, assigning specific meanings to how someone behaves. However, we would tend to avoid the generalised 'this body language means that and that body language means this'. Like all language, the context will affect the meaning and certain postures and gestures may mean different things depending on the situation. This will be true for the speaker as well as the audience. A member of the audience with arms folded may be perfectly receptive, just a bit chilly. Or perhaps they are more comfortable with arms folded.

However, some combinations of body language may send signals to the audience, intended or otherwise. Some body language is simply distracting and off-putting. Consider the difference between a speaker who is confident and a speaker who is not. What do they look like? What differences might you notice?

Ineffective Body Language

Here are some physiological behaviours that are generally best avoided when presenting and training:

- Pacing up and down (like a caged zoo animal)
- Swaying and rocking back and forth
- Dancing from side to side, forwards and backwards (the 'square dance').
- Standing off balance (for example with one leg behind the other)
- Both hands in pocket, jingling keys etc. Hands in and out of pockets may result in the pocket or contents of pocket poking out!
- Focussing on the screen or flipchart instead of the audience. Facing away from the audience (hence with one's back to them).
- Fixating on one member of the audience or on one side of the room and hence not making eye contact with others.
- 'Space Invading': Standing too close to the audience, talking over the top of the front rows.
- 'Space Evading': Standing behind the audience (or too far off to one side) and talking.
- Over protecting oneself, with arms folded or standing with hands covering the 'lower regions' (also known as the 'fig leaf' stance).

The Model Presenter

Effective Body Language

- Keeping feet planted, then when needing to move, moving purposefully from one place to another.
- Standing/sitting with a strong stance, upright, shoulders back and chest up whilst relaxed (also known as the 'star' stance).
- Maintaining stillness with purposeful animation.
- Using gestures to 'place' items and messages or to indicate a sequence/process (known as 'spatial anchoring').
- Looking around the audience, making brief eye contact with everyone at some point (also known as the 'lighthouse effect').
- Smiling (as appropriate!)
- Using natural and expressive gestures and expressions.

Purposeful Voice

Voice includes our tonality and all of our vocal behaviours:

- *Pace*: How quickly or slowly do you speak? Are you able to vary the speed consciously?
- *Volume*: How loud or quiet are you?
- *Pitch*: How high or low do you speak? How much variation do you have?
- *Clarity*: How clear or muffled is the sound of your voice?
- *Timbre & Resonance*: How strong is your voice? What is the quality of the sound you make? Is there a 'vibration' in your voice?
- *Accent*: What accent do you have? Are you proud of your accent? Can you shift accents when you want to?
- *Emphasis*: Are you able to put more 'oomph' into certain words to highlight them as important?
- *Pauses*: Do you use pauses to create an effect or to indicate a shift of one topic to another?

Have you noticed that some voices are easier to listen to than others? Some you can listen to for hours and others cause a mental switching off after just a few moments. As a member of the audience, it is sometimes hard to stay interested in someone who sounds bored with themselves or the message they are delivering. Consider a confident voice and a non-confident voice... how do they sound different? What distinguishes one from the other?

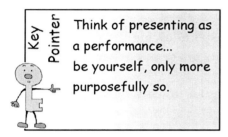

Key Pointer

Think of presenting as a performance...

be yourself, only more purposefully so.

The art of utilising your voice is to act a little like you are performing. Bring a bit of drama to your presentations and training. If your normal speaking voice is 100%, you will find that most people prefer that you perform at 150% (unless you are already blessed with a powerful and purposeful voice!) Listen to actors and mimic them (in the comfort of your own home/car if you like). The idea here is not to become them or be an

impressionist, but to give yourself a stronger range in your voice. Play with and practice speaking at different pitches, speeds and volumes. Test out different accents (alone if needs be!) If you want to learn more about how to vary and control your voice, get some singing lessons or voice coaching.

Some of the ineffective voice examples below may be challenging for a person to change, particularly if they have had that voice for years and it is part of their identity. What we are advocating here is to learn to stretch your voice, to give yourself more variety. Your 'natural' voice is not who you are; you are so much more than that!

The Model Presenter

Ineffective Voice

Here are some things to avoid unless you are purposefully playing for effect:

- *Monotone*: Some people speak in a single tone with no differentiation or emphasis. This can sound robotic and is hard to listen to for any length of time. Monotone is monotonous!
- *Mumbling*: When a presenter doesn't allowing the words out of their mouth, it can be hard to make out what they are saying.
- *Too quiet*: Some people have a quiet voice which might be fine in close-up conversation. However, if an audience cannot hear what the speaker is saying, there is little point them being there (neither speaker nor audience!)
- *Too loud*: Whilst a loud speaker can be heard, the intense volume can be distracting (or possibly painful!) Some people do not seem able to adjust their volume to the size of the room or group. A booming voice is great in a large hall, but off putting in a small meeting room.
- *Too fast*: One of the classic signs of a nervous presenter! When someone delivers their whole presentation too quickly, it may appear as if they just want to get out of there. Of course, speed can indicate excitement and being upbeat... however, if this continues throughout, it can become hard to listen to.
- *Whiney*: Some people talk as if they are constantly complaining about something even when they are not. Sometimes there is a 'nasal' quality to the voice that begins to grate after a while.
- *Harsh*: Some presenters speak with a somewhat discordant voice, perhaps sounding like 'Dalek' from Doctor Who. This can make the speaker sound unintentionally comical or at worse rather stupid.

- *Drifting off*: We have noticed that some presenters start each sentence strong but then their voice 'drops off' at the end. By quietening at the end, the audience begin to lose part of what is being said and so they begin to lose interest. There is also something rather hypnotic about this pattern of speaking so the audience may also begin to 'trance out'!
- *Going up*: A speaker who consistently goes up at the end of each sentence (known as 'upward inflection') can appear unsure of what they are saying. There are certain accents and teenage affectations that play out this pattern, however, they may be missing an opportunity to make credible statements or add gravitas to their message.

Effective Voice

- *Purposeful*: Choose how you use your voice to enhance your message. On occasion, you might even use some of the above ineffective voice types at an appropriate moment for effect; perhaps you might use them as an example or to make a point.
- *Variety*: Use a range of speeds to reflect what you are talking about. Allow the pace to reflect the emotion. Within reason, range the pitch of your voice. Remember that a higher pitch at the end of a sentence tends to indicate a question and is more likely to invite a response from the audience. Voice down at the end adds extra credibility and certainly. Level at the end indicates 'normal' statements.
- *Volume*: Use volume to captivate an audience, from strong and loud when appropriate to barely a whisper (as long as people can still hear you).
- *Emphasis*: Slow it down a bit, put more oomph into certain words. This will help to pick out key words for the audience and make your message easier to process. Outside of presenting, play with putting emphasis on different words in a statement and notice what effect it has. For example, say the following statement a few times, putting emphasis on

different words (or a different word) each time: "I shall deliver this presentation with style".

- *Emotionality*: Emotions affect the voice. When we are truly feeling something, our voice reflects it. If you are speaking of something exciting or happy or relaxing, let your voice reflect that.
- *Squeezing words*: Use your voice to sound out the meaning of a word. For example saying 'squeeze' and if you are 'sque-e-e-z-ing' it out. Say 'slow' slowly, say 'soft' softly, say 'wonder' as if in awe of the word.
- *Accent*: Whilst you might want to be careful not to mimic your audience in a disrespectful way, having a range of accents in your repertoire can help to give some extra variety to a longer presentation. Accents can be effectively used for certain phrases or quotations rather than over a longer period.

The Impact of Body Language on Your Voice

Have you ever noticed the difference in your voice when you are standing up versus sitting down? Standing tends to bring about a more assertive, credible voice and sitting a gentler, softer, more empathetic voice. This will also depend on your stance of course. Try talking with your shoulders collapsed and hunched; then with your shoulders back and posture straighter. As discussed below, when you stand with your chest higher and your shoulders back, you are taking on the posture of confidence.

How do you sound differently when your body is tense and when your body is relaxed? Give it a go! Stand or sit with tension in your body, particularly your chest and neck, and then talk. Then shake it out and sit or stand comfortably. Now notice how your voice sounds.

Your voice will tend to strengthen when you use stronger gestures. You might have noticed politicians speaking whilst using a cutting/chopping motion with their hand... this helps them to emphasise and punctuate what they are saying. Alternatively, it may give a brief rhythm to their emphasis, allowing them to make a series of points. For example: "Over the next four years we must improve services [*chop one*], cut taxes [*chop two*], cut unnecessary spending [*chop three*] and above all make this country a country to be proud of [*big chop four*]".

Getting the Audience's Attention

Imagine the moment just before the start of a presentation where the audience is talking to one another. Or perhaps the audience has been doing a paired exercise or small group discussion. You want to get their attention and bring them 'back to the room'. Depending on the size of the audience, how do you make yourself heard? How do you command such a presence physically that the audience know it is time to stop? If you have a microphone and speakers, this should be an easier task, but what if you don't?

The following ideas will work differently depending on the type and/or size of the group. With some of the them, it is worth letting the group know *how* you are going to get their attention back so they know what to listen out for. As you make the sound, make your body language bigger, e.g. stand with your arms (or just one arm) up and outstretched. Use your hands to beckon people back (as if you are guiding an ocean liner!) Obviously there are certain ways of doing this which could look ridiculous, so use some common sense... look in the mirror and test it out if necessary!

- *Clapping*: This can be a quick way of getting the attention of the group back as long as you can clap relatively loudly!
- *Whistle*: Either using a whistle or by whistling. We would avoid the referee type whistle since it is too sharp and shrill. A friend of ours uses a whistle that sounds like an old train

whistle, loud but pleasing to the ear. Whistling randomly (for example like a songbird) gets people's attention too!

- *Shushing*: A loud shushing noise that gets quieter can also be effective, although it may come across as a bit parental or teacher like. Our preference is to entertain the group rather than make them feel like they are six years old!
- *'Piercing voice'*: This is something to practise. You will find that without shouting, you can project your voice (like an actor). Certain pitches will have a stronger resonance, as will certain sounds. For example, the end of the word 'okay' if said slowly has an 'eeye' sound which can pierce through the chatter of an audience. As an exercise, sing some scales and notice at which pitch your voice is strongest. Try out some different words and sounds.
- *Chimes*: A bell can be useful, particularly the more pleasant sounding chimes (e.g. wind chimes or Tibetan bells). We would not use an old school bell though... just our preference!
- *Music*: If you have access to a sound system, stick some music on to bring people back! (Make sure the venue is licensed to use music.)

Once you have people's attention, or have got the majority, be ready to say something that captures and captivates the audience again. Make them want to listen to you as opposed to talking to each other.

Body and Emotion

There are times when training and presenting that you will want to influence and/or manage the emotions of the group. The first step in doing this is in handling your own emotions. What if you could become purposeful with your emotions, moving from state to state at will?

Managing Your Own Emotions

Whilst Chapter 12 is dedicated to handling nervousness and anxiety, what about other emotions? Which emotions would you like to experience more of when you are presenting?

Excitement   Motivation   Contentment
Confidence   Joy   Reflectivity
Relaxation   Calmness   Humour   Laughter

How do you access emotions? The easiest starting point is to write down examples of when, where and with whom you experience certain emotions. Emotions can be triggered by people, places, activities and events. So grab a note pad and write down some examples of when/where you feel/felt any of the emotions listed above. Feel free to add any others you like. Sometimes a little bit of anger can be useful too, especially when it is used in observational humour!

Consider for each of the emotions you have written about, what does each one do for you? How does it serve you and in what circumstances might it be useful? This will help you to find the most appropriate emotion for each context you are talking about or that you find yourself in.

When you experience an emotion, notice what it is like. Where do you feel it (in your body)? What sort of temperature is it? How intense it is? What thoughts or words go with it (if any)? By becoming familiar with your emotions, you are more likely to be able to switch from one to another purposefully, like a good actor.

Another method of accessing emotion is through your body language. Not only do emotions affect your body language, but your body will also affect your emotions. The two things are inextricably interlinked. As mentioned earlier in the chapter, confidence tends to correlate with your chest being up and your shoulders being back. Excitement is associated with movement. Notice in yourself and others, the postures, gestures, movement and facial expressions of different emotions. Become more purposeful in your body language (and voice) to create and/or reflect the emotions you wish to utilise.

Managing Emotions in Others

You will find some ideas in chapter 11 on how to manage 'difficult' emotions in a group, but what if you want the audience to feel a particular emotion?

In the same way that you access emotions for yourself, the same is likely to be true for most members of an audience. Start by getting yourself into a low level of the emotion you want the audience to experience. For example, if you want the audience to feel motivated, you need to get a sense of motivation yourself. This doesn't have to be a full blown emotional state right away; indeed this might put the audience off. By feeling a sense of the emotion and then gradually building it, this helps the audience to come with you.

Get the audience into positive emotional states by having them associate to people, places, activities and events. Talk about your own experiences and have them talk about their own. Use examples and stories of other people who have done amazing things or have overcome less than easy situations.

Use your voice and body language to convey emotion. Slow things down or speed them up. Increase or decrease the volume of your voice or the size of your gestures. Change the pitch, higher for excitement or surprise and lower for gravitas and importance.

In a practical sense, in order to manage the emotions of the group constructively, make sure that you have at least two activities in a 90 minute period (i.e. get the audience involved or doing/discussing something in smaller groups). If you are running for more than minutes, make sure there is a comfort break.

Model Making

As a model presenter:

- Gather feedback about the impact of your body language and voice
- Become more purposeful with your body, voice and emotional state
- Get familiar with the body language, voice and state of confidence

The Model Presenter

Chapter 8

Language: Engaging the Audience

In This Chapter...

In this chapter, you will discover how language impacts on the Mind of the audience. We will reveal to you some of the hidden layers of language and hence how to be more purposeful with what you say. You will learn how to guide an audience with your words and develop your ability to motivate and inspire.

We will be exploring the following questions:

- What is the direct impact of language on the brain?
- What are some examples of language to use and to avoid?
- What makes language compelling, engaging and multisensory?
- What is 'you' language and how can you use it more purposefully?
- What presuppositions are hidden in your language?
- What is 'signposting', why is it important and how do you do it?

The Impact of Language

Think of a giraffe. We don't know what kind of a giraffe you will imagine... perhaps a picture or a video of a moving giraffe. It might be a giraffe you have seen before or a made up one. It may even be a cartoon giraffe. And it may have been each of those different things as you read the words there.

The Model Presenter

At any given moment in time, each word we use and the relationship between those words will have a consequence at a physical, sensory level. Every word that has a meaning to us will fire off a set of corresponding neurons in our brain. For example, assuming we have learnt the word 'giraffe' and given it meaning (i.e. related it to something), when we experience the word 'giraffe', a network of neural associations will 'light up' (generating internal pictures, sounds, thoughts and related words/concepts). Then, depending on what feeling that network stimulates (e.g. like, dislike, neutral), we will have a physiological reaction. For instance, if someone is very fond of giraffes and they experience the word 'giraffe', they may get a warm, fuzzy feeling inside.

Bottom line... language has a direct impact on our neurology (and hence our physiology, thinking and emotions).

Getting the Audience Tied up in 'Nots'

Be aware that negations (e.g. 'not'/'don't' type words) have a sometimes unintended neurological effect on the mind of the audience. For example, don't think of that very giraffe you thought of just now. What happens? Most people think of the giraffe again. Now, whatever you do, don't think of an elephant...

How do some trainers and presenters get what they *don't* want? They focus on what they *don't* want the audience to do! For example they might say "I don't want you to get confused here" or "don't talk about this for too long" or "don't worry".

Imagine the brain acts like an advanced internet search engine. If you type 'not giraffe' into a search engine, what happens? It doesn't bring up the rest of the internet (i.e. every website that doesn't mention giraffes); it comes up with all the websites that reference giraffes! Of course, the brain is even smarter than that because it also comes up with things it has associated with giraffes, e.g. zoo, long neck, tall leafy trees, antelopes, big animals.

By saying "don't worry", the brain of each individual in the audience accesses 'worry' (since it fires off the neural network associated with the word and concept of 'worry'). Another way of thinking about it is that no matter where the brain goes to search, it has only 'worry' as its reference point.

The Common Tongue

Perhaps it is a cliché by now, but it is important to use the language of the audience (unless you are purposefully doing otherwise... more about that in a moment). Not only does this mean that the audience is more likely to understand you, but it will help to build and maintain rapport (as you work from the mind of the audience). Use their jargon and buzzwords, or at the very least, use the 'common tongue'. If you use your own jargon or 'academic', scientific words that the audience is unfamiliar with, guess what happens? Less neurons fire in the brains of the listeners and they get bored.

For example, this is taken from a random power-point presentation slide off the internet[1]: "For ab initio or DFT calculations, many programs require a basis set choice to be made." Most audience members without the background knowledge would hear and process this as something like: "For blah-blah or blah-blah-blah calculations, many blah-blah require a blah-blah-blah-blah to be made".

Of course, there might be times you will want to purposefully use some different language. You might need to mismatch the group to differentiate yourself from the mind of the audience. You might be teaching the group new ideas where they need to learn new terminology. You might also use different language if the group has gone into a negative place and you want to move them on.

The Model Presenter

Lost in Translation

We have noticed that for people who are multilingual, they are best off preparing a presentation in the language that they are going to deliver it. We had an example of a trainer from Denmark who prepared his presentations in Danish and then translated as he presented. Not only was this a little awkward but the structure of the language was odd. When he prepared in English to deliver in English, he was excellent.

Apparently, different languages reflect their culture[2] (or perhaps vice versa). For example, if one of us knocked over a vase and it broke we would say: "I broke the vase" (unless we were a politician and we might say: "The vase was broken"!) However, in Spanish, the translation would be: "The vase broke itself" and according to an Italian friend of ours, in Italian the translation would be: "I suffered the vase being broken". Interesting!

Strong and Colourful Language

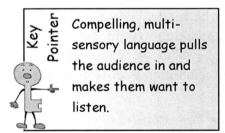

Key Pointer

Compelling, multi-sensory language pulls the audience in and makes them want to listen.

Of course, when we refer to strong and colourful language we are not talking here about expletives and naughty rudeness! We are talking about strong and compelling language as opposed to weak, dull neutral language. We are talking about colourful language as opposed to grey, robotic language.

Compelling Language

If weak language includes words like 'quite', 'nice', 'good', 'all right' and 'fine', what would strong compelling language include? Some of the most compelling language is positive, active and descriptive.

Words like 'compelling', 'magnetic', 'excellent', 'powerful', 'inspired' and 'passionate'.

<table>
<tr><td rowspan="7" style="writing-mode:vertical-lr">A Case In Point</td><td>We have noticed a trend for presenters to announce near the beginning of their presentation: "I am going to talk to you about..." Whilst this is not dreadful, consider what it does in the mind of the audience. It does sound rather one way, as if the presenter is going to be talking *at* an audience who will be sitting there passively. This phrase may run the risk of switching the audience off and hence increases the 'gap' between the presenter and audience.</td></tr>
</table>

Given that the goal for the presenter is to close the gap, what might be some effective ways of telling the audience what you are going to be covering? Here are some suggestions taken from different perspectives:

I focus	We focus	You focus
I will be covering	We will be covering	You will discover
I will be revealing	We will be exploring	You will experience
I'd like to share	We will be discussing	You will develop

As a presenter, it is worth broadening your speaking vocabulary. Write some compelling words down and use them purposefully until they become second nature. Here are some examples to get you started:

accomplished	energetic	imaginative	passionate	sparkling
adaptable	engaging	important	peaceful	special
authentic	enlightened	impressive	powerful	spontaneous
balanced	entertaining	influential	precious	successful
bright	enthusiastic	inspired	profound	superb
brilliant	excellent	intelligent	purposeful	tender
captivating	extraordinary	intuitive	radiant	tranquil
daring	fascinating	inventive	real	unique
decisive	flexible	joyful	receptive	versatile

The Model Presenter

determined	focused	knowledgeable	relaxed	virtuous
ecstatic	healthy	lucid	remarkable	wonderful
elegant	heroic	magnetic	serene	
encouraging	humorous	natural	sincere	

Flexible Language

Some presenters/trainers seem to think that strong, powerful language is about making sweeping statements and insisting that they are right; or perhaps that it means taking a position on something and arguing aggressively with the audience! In fact, it appears as if the opposite is true. Strength is about flexibility.

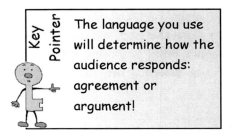

Key Pointer
The language you use will determine how the audience responds: agreement or argument!

Indeed, absolute statements tend to make some of the audience want to disagree. (*Notice we didn't say that "absolute statements will make the audience disagree" which would be relatively easy to disagree with!*) A presenter can save themselves a fair amount of grief by using flexible language... the language of possibility. Here we are suggesting rather than telling. We are offering rather than insisting. We are owning our opinion rather than presenting it as fact.

Here are some other examples of flexible, possibility words:

It seems	Some (e.g. people)	Tend to	Relatively
It appears	Sometimes	May	Somewhat
It could be	Often	Might	Almost
argued	Most	Could	Possibly
	A lot of	Can	Kind of

Of course, too much possibility language can come across as weak, particularly to an audience who want it 'black and white' (i.e. is it or isn't it). However, when it comes to talking about people and organisations there are very few absolute truths! In the same vein, it is worth avoiding phrases like 'they say' or 'scientists have proven' as if this makes your case for you. Either give your references to the research you are referring to or use words like research 'suggests' (rather than 'proves'). Of course, this is your choice and it depends what you are training and presenting. However, if you find you get a lot of argumentative audiences... then consider your own language!

Multisensory Language

In terms of colourful language, we mean 'multisensory'. Humans are physical creatures; everything we understand and process is done so through our five senses... so *engage* the senses of the audience. Here are some examples of sensory words and phrases[3]:

Visual (Sight)	Auditory (Hearing)	Kinesthetic (Feeling)	Olfactory & Gustatory (Smell & Taste)
See	Hear what you say	Gut feeling	Food for thought
Picture	Sounds good	Under pressure	Smell of success
Look	Dropped a clanger	On top of it	Taster
Clearer	Rings a bell	Touch	Bitter aftertaste
Clouding over	Off with a bang	Strong	Sweeten the deal
Perspective	Squeaky clean	Handle	Smell a rat
Colourful character	That jars	Heavy	Whiff
Bleak prospect	What a row	Comfortable	Smells fishy
Dark secret	Music to my ears	Weak link	Flavour
Shed some light	Echoes of the past	High	Juicy
Looking ahead	Say to myself	Tense	Fruitful
Brighten up	Sound as a bell	Step	Scent
Scene	In tune	Weight	Spicy
My view	Harmonious	On edge	Appetite
Focus	Strikes a chord	Grasp	Savour
Look up to	Screech to a halt	Grab	A nose for it

Mind Your Language

Where do you want to take the audience with your words? Do you want them in the middle of what you are talking about or do you want to distance them from it?

Most presenters do not realise what they are doing with their language. They may want the audience engaged and involved but the language they are using holds the audience at bay.

Imagine that you are listening to someone giving directions. Consider the following:

1. "The building is twenty meters from the car park. The reception area is through the main doors. In the reception area the stairs are on the left hand side and there are four floors in total. On the third floor is a double doorway and there is an office through the doorway, along the corridor and second to the right. That is the location of the meeting."

2. "From the car park, you'll find reception through the main doors. You will see some stairs on the left, so go on up to the third floor. You will then need to go through a double door and then into the second office on the left. I'll see you there for the meeting."

The likelihood is that you will experience the first set of directions from a remote perspective. Although factual, they may come across as 'dull'. They may be logical but this kind of language can be harder to follow – especially if used in a lengthier presentation.

You are more likely to experience the second description from your own perspective as if you are going on that journey to the office on the third floor. Chances are (depending on the voice of the speaker) you would have found the second description lighter, possibly more in focus and easier to follow and to remember. Even if this is not an exact match to your experience, the point is that the language we use will tend to affect the listener's internal experiences/perspectives and hence how they process and store what you are saying.

If this was part of a longer presentation, most people would find the 'you' description more compelling and engaging. So, when you are presenting information, do you want the audience to feel associated to what you are saying or disassociated... in the picture or removed from it?

<u>The Impact of Pronouns</u>

The pronouns you use will tend to affect the perspective of the audience. By changing who the subject of your 'story' is, you will change the way the audience experiences it:

Pronoun	Impact
I	Some personal stories and examples can help to build rapport and empathy with the audience. It can bring a touch of 'humanness'. However, too much 'I' can become a little tedious and egotistical!
You	By making the audience the subject of your examples and situations, you engage and associate them into 'being there'. Over a period of time, 'you' language is easier to listen to.
He/She They	Using a 'third person' perspective creates a picture of someone else doing something. If the story is engaging enough (even if it is about a thing), the audience may still process the story and put themselves 'in it' from time to time to make sense of the story.
We	We 'inclusive' (i.e. the speaker and listener in it together) can build a sense of 'we are on the same side and in it together'. If this is we 'exclusive' (i.e. the speaker and his/her own group) then it can help to build credibility when used in moderation (for example: "We carried out this research").
It	The third person objective language of 'it' can generate some credibility and is the style of the objective scientist. However, it is rather disassociated and can become boring and hard to listen to if used for too long.

Associated vs Disassociated Language

You might want to associate your audience to something when you want them to feel connected and engaged with it. You might want to disassociate your audience from something you want them to distance/detach themselves from. As well as using pronouns, here are some other examples of words that associate/disassociate:

Associated	Disassociated
Here	There
Now	Then
This/These	That/Those
Is	Was

If you want to bring something into the mind of the client/audience, you might say: "This road we are on together here and now is our new direction" and to distance from the old way of doing things: "...because that old path was how things were back there and then and is for those people who would not adapt."

Accidental 'You' Language

We have noticed that when people are talking about problems, they tend to change (often unconsciously) from 'I' to 'you'[4]. For example: "I went to see my manager to explain why I had to go early, and then it's like 'bang', suddenly you're on his naughty list". The speaker has been describing the story from their own perspective and has then switched to 'you' language. It could be that we do this to disassociate ourselves from the difficulty. However, it means we are 'putting it on' the listener as we 'put them in' the situation! In some languages, negative 'you' language is considered rude.

Other people we meet seem to throw away all the good stuff. They might be talking about something they achieved and as soon as they get to the feeling proud or happy, they say: "I did X, Y and Z and, you know, you feel really good for doing it". Whilst this is very kind, it means the speaker is disassociating from the good feelings and praise they are due. They are not owning 'feeling good'.

> **A Case In Point**
>
> Someone we know has a habit of saying: "so there you are" or "so there you go" after bemoaning his medical conditions. It is as if he is listing out his ailments and then unconsciously trying to pass them over to someone else. If you find yourself in the company of unresourceful 'you' language, imagine there is a 'flexi-glass' screen in front of you and all those negative statements are bouncing off and away from you!

Purposeful Language

We encourage you to become aware of your own speech patterns and in particular your 'you' language. Where necessary, own your own experience with 'I'. If you are talking about a less than positive state or expounding a limiting belief, then you might use 'some people' instead of 'you', e.g. instead of: "It's hard doing presentations, don't you find?", use something like: "I think some people find it less than easy to do presentations".

In addition take responsibility for the images you want to create in your audience. Become more purposeful with your language. Where do you intend to take them with what you say?

'You' language can also become 'installation' language, full of 'embedded suggestions' that we are constantly giving out to others (e.g. "I know you can do this because *you are excellent* at this kind of thing" where 'you are excellent' is the embedded suggestion). If some of our 'you' language is less than resourceful, we are linguistically placing our audience in unresourceful situations and hence doing them a disservice. To counter this, by talking in 'positive outcome' language you can 'gift' others[5] with hundreds of positive embedded suggestions and resources! This makes you a compelling person to be with and to listen to.

If you would like to be known as an engaging (e.g.) presenter, trainer, partner, leader or friend, then whenever you speak, make sure that what you say is directed towards 'what is wanted and needed' instead of away from 'what is problematic/wrong'. When you use 'you' language under these circumstances, people will think that *you are positive and empowering*.

The Answer is in the Question

When we talk to others there will be certain things that are presupposed in what we say. If someone says: "I'll see you at the meeting", this statement presupposes:

- There is a meeting
- They are going to the meeting
- You are going to the meeting
- They can see (and you will be visible)!

Now, imagine that you are running a workshop and the audience has come back from doing an exercise. You want to debrief it and get some feedback. Consider the difference between these questions:

1. Did that go well?
2. How did that go?
3. How well did that go?
4. What did you do well?

The first question is closed and encourages a yes/no answer. Don't blame the group for being unreceptive if this is the question you ask! The second question encourages some evaluation, both 'positive' and 'negative'. The third question focuses the group towards evaluating what went well and presupposes that things did go well. The fourth question encourages the group to give examples of what they did and presupposes that they did some things well.

How does knowing the difference between those questions help you? It allows you to ask questions in a variety of ways to get the group thinking differently. *(And how does that question: 'how does knowing the difference between those questions help you?' differ from: 'does knowing the difference between those questions help you?' It presupposes that the questions are helpful and we are just asking 'in what way?')*

So...was that useful? *How was that useful?* Do you get the difference? *How do you get the difference...* etc.

<u>Beware of What You are Saying in What You Are Not Saying!</u>

Some presenters have a habit of putting themselves down or acting as if their subject is boring or their presentation doesn't matter... without even realising they are doing it. In the same way that there are positive, encouraging presuppositions, there can also be negative and limiting ones too. Consider what a speaker is suggesting unconsciously to the audience when he/she asks: "Can you hold questions for the end so I can get through this presentation?" Might it suggest that the presenter doesn't really want to be there and would like to get done as soon as possible?

What do the following suggest to you?

- I won't bore you with details about myself.
- I'll just quickly present some of the ideas.
- I'll try not to send you to sleep with this data.

If a speaker isn't careful they can undermine their credibility and make it look as if they do not want to be there. If the audience picks up on this, they may make the speaker *really* wish they weren't there!

Signposting and Meaning Making

Every presentation needs to have a 'context frame', i.e. what it is about, how it is relevant and why it is important. In addition, the audience needs to know:

a) *Where are we?* As you move from topic to topic, sub-topic to sub-topic and point to point within your presentation, it is helpful to let the audience know where they are and where they are going to next. This can be done with **signposting**, which is a bit like providing headings and subheadings in something you might be writing.

b) *What does this mean?* Any information you provide needs to be put into a frame in order for it to mean something and to have relevance to the audience. This can be done by 'meaning making', which creates links between your material and the experience of the audience.

a) Where Are We? Signposting

Imagine a business book without any headings or subheadings... perhaps no paragraph breaks either. A book like that would soon become confusing and hard to follow. Presentations are the same.

During your presentation, whether you are using visual aids or not, it is helpful to 'signpost' where you are in the 'agenda'. As an audience member, there is something psychologically comforting in knowing how far into the presentation you are and how long there is left... even when you are enjoying it.

Once you have moved beyond the introduction phase, for each key area it is worth stating the title of the section you are about to cover and then giving a benefit to the audience of this key area. For example: "Okay, so we begin with 'rapport'. How would it be to broaden the amount of people you can connect with when you first meet them?" or "Okay, so let's move on to the budget for this year. This will help you to focus on what's really important and to prioritise your spending."

From one sentence to the next, pause a little and breathe. From one 'paragraph'/segment to the next, take a slightly longer pause. For each subheading you might use words like 'okay, so...' and then give the 'title' of the next part. For a change in topic, you might take a break (e.g. on a course) or say 'okay so moving on to the next section'. If you are using power-point, have a 'signpost' slide that gives the title of the next section.

If you are talking about a process and there are a series of steps in the process, make sure the audience is clear about which step you are on, for example: "Okay, so the first step is... And then moving on to the second step..." Of course, if you say 'first step', this presupposes there will be at least a second one. By numbering the steps in a process, you are giving the audience a sense of quantified structure which can also add credibility to what you are saying. If you mention a 'first' or 'step/point one', remember to maintain your credibility by signposting 'second' and 'third' or steps/points 'two' and 'three'.

Another method of signposting involves asking a question and then answering it, for example: "So, how many people achieved their targets last year? The breakdown is as follows..."

There may be times when you (or the audience) have strayed and you want to bring it back or move on to the next subject area. You can linguistically 'signpost' to the audience that this is the time. For example: "Okay, so back to the story line!" or "Okay, so moving on then!"

Sometimes, you may need to refer to a sub-topic that you will be returning to later, for example: "This is also relevant to project management and I will be coming on to that in a few minutes". If it is a question or comment from the audience that refers to something you will be speaking about later you might say something like: "Great question... you're ahead of the game... hold that thought, we'll be coming back to it in a little while."

b) What does that mean? Making meaning

Data without a frame or context is meaningless. If you are presented with the data "34% and 38%", this means nothing without more information around it. Even with the 'fact' that "34% of people are dissatisfied and 38% are satisfied", there is still not enough information to create any relevance. If we know that the context is the most recent staff survey and the percentages are linked to how satisfied people are with their manager's performance, this begins to help, but still does not tell us how this compares to the year before, or how this compares to other companies. Is this good or bad?

When someone presents pure data, it may be neither relevant nor interesting to the audience. How might you give data meaning? Here are some ways of putting your data into a context:

- Compare the data with something else (e.g. the length of the building is about 200 meters... which is like two football pitches end to end).
- Go from an individual example to the data to the big picture (e.g. an inoculation costing £10 can help to save a person's life... we have raised £1000... helping to save 100 lives).
- Funnel from the big picture to your data (e.g. surveys across companies in the UK suggest that an average of 25% of staff are satisfied with their manager's performance; our most recent staff survey tells us that 38% of people in this company are satisfied with their manager's performance).

Model Making

As a model presenter:

- Become aware of the impact of your language
- Develop a more positive vocabulary
- Use language to create the experiences you want the audience to have in mind
- Let the audience know where you are through 'signposting'

The Model Presenter

Chapter 9

Examples, Stories and Metaphors

In This Chapter...

In this chapter, you will find out more about the use of examples, stories and metaphors in your delivery and how they can enhance your message. You will also learn a little bit about the psychology behind using stories.

We will be exploring the following questions:

- What do examples, stories and metaphors do for an audience?
- Why would you want to use stories... how do they help you?
- How might you use stories to enhance your message?

Modelling Examples, Stories and Metaphors

<u>Why examples stories and metaphors?</u>

Have you ever been to a really 'dry' presentation that became hard to listen to after a short while? It may have been perfectly credible, with models and theories backed up with facts and figures, and yet it failed to grab your attention. It may have been full of data demonstrated in spreadsheets, pie-charts, graphs and percentages, but you ended up with information overload.

Dry presentations are usually the result of a lack of examples. Without examples, there is no real world application or opportunity for the audience to make meaning out of the data. In addition, there is no opportunity for the audience to feel connected to you as the speaker. By giving personal examples, whether they be specific applications of your material, or whether they be real personal stories that make a point of some kind, you will help to 'close the gap' between yourself and the audience.

Examples and stories bring a presentation or training alive. The key difference between an engaging presentation and a mediocre one is the stories that relate the listener back to their own experience. Not only do stories add colour and brightness to an otherwise dull and lifeless presentation, they can help to clarify your material in the mind of the audience and help them apply the material back to their real worlds.

Overall, examples, stories and metaphors can be useful to:

- Set a context or frame.
- Clarify a point.
- Allow for easier application.
- Elicit desired states in the audience.
- Enhance or change the state of the audience
- Suggest a possible solution to an audience.
- Discourage an audience from taking particular routes or behaving in particular ways.

What are examples, stories and metaphors?

Whilst there is an overlap between examples, stories and metaphors, it may be useful to make some distinctions:

a) Examples

Examples are often factual and based on the data you are presenting. They make data easier to understand by demonstrating real world application. Consider the difference here:

- *Data without an example*: "87% of staff scored the management as 'trustworthy' in the recent staff satisfaction survey."
- *Data with an example*: "87% of staff scored the management as 'trustworthy' in the recent staff satisfaction survey. An example here is a member of staff who added the comment that their manager helped them to secure some training that was not core to their job role, but helped them think about next steps in their career."

The data with example allows the audience to get a clearer idea of what 'trustworthy' means to the staff and gives an indicator to other managers as to what they might think about doing.

Examples might also be cautionary, highlighting problems as well as solutions, e.g. in a presentation about customer satisfaction targets: "Some people are still using the old system to process payments, but this is leading to a delay in distribution and hence unhappy customers." In this situation, the example may be being used to set the frame for a discussion.

Where possible, it is useful to give examples about people the audience can relate to. For example, you might refer to a previous group you were training/presenting to... "I was working with a group recently and they did X" or "someone from a previous group said he dealt with situation Y in this way and it worked well for him".

b) Stories

The best kinds of story are those that are relevant to the material and relevant to the audience. Of course, some stories may not, on the surface, seem relevant (perhaps being rather metaphorical – see below) but it is helpful if they have some purpose or bearing on the occasion!

Some stories may be used to change or enhance the state or mood of the audience, but these are still relevant - even if the audience doesn't know it! For example, when we are training, we might tell an associated story to make the audience laugh and smile. Whilst the story in and of itself may not *appear* to bear a relevant message, it might relax the audience or help them back into an enjoying/learning state.

Stories may help the audience to achieve something, by providing psychological resources (e.g. confidence) and practical, "how-to" tips and steps. Stories can also prime an audience not to do something. This is known as inoculation: framing a particular behaviour or activity as unwanted or unhelpful. If you are teaching people how to climb a ladder safely, you might tell them about the guy who dropped his paint pot because his ladder wasn't properly secured. Safe driving classes will often go further to point out how a case of carelessness led to injury or fatality.

A Case In Point

A few years ago, on a corporate trainer's training course, I had a health and safety trainer who wouldn't use examples and stories. It was all just data and process and dreadfully boring. I said: "Surely you must have some interesting stories of where things went wrong... perhaps of people doing stupid and dangerous things? These would be the things you want people to avoid doing." He replied that he was there to deliver facts, not stories and couldn't (or wouldn't) see the point of examples like that. I said: "Fine, but be prepared for the audience to find it less than engaging."

Often, the most powerful stories are your own, i.e. things that have happened to you in your own life. However, stories can effectively be borrowed from others (e.g. "I was told a story once about..." or "I read an article recently that said...") or can be stories about others (e.g. "I knew a guy who..."). When you are borrowing a story from another source, it is usually best to acknowledge where it came from, or that it is someone else's story. There is nothing worse than a presenter/trainer speaking as if they themselves did or experienced something that you know was really someone else. Plagiarising stories without referencing is a high risk strategy and can ruin the credibility of the speaker if they are found out. It can be on a par with a presenter stealing someone else's idea and presenting it as their own.

c) Metaphors

<u>*i. Metaphor allows for multiple meanings*</u>
Metaphor, as used here, is a generic term for one thing representing another, akin to an analogy. A story, if treated metaphorically, allows for a range of interpretations. In this sense, it is up to the listener to decide the meaning, either consciously or unconsciously. Because the listener becomes part of the process of interpreting a metaphorical story, you are not imposing a specific message or learning point, merely suggesting it.

Using metaphor appears to be a way of distancing ourselves from a situation or problem. If we say that an issue is like the left hand not knowing what the right hand is doing, we convey a message of perceived confusion. In this instance, the speaker can use metaphorical language rather than express specific feelings of e.g. frustration about specific named people not communicating with each other. It seems that speaking metaphorically is sometimes a 'safer' way of communicating.

In addition, when we hear metaphorical stories about other people's problems, they often seem easier to solve than our own problems. However, if the other person's situation matches or represents our problem, it may give us enough distance to have insights into solving our own problem.

The Model Presenter

As well as perhaps helping someone to resolve a problem, we might also use metaphorical language to help the audience understand a concept. For example, if we are trying to explain organisational culture, we might describe it as like an onion where you can peel away one layer and find another underneath. This might lead to the introduction of a model which allows for exploration of the multiple layers of the organisational culture

ii. The 'reality – fantasy' scale

One way of approaching metaphor is to consider the 'reality – fantasy' scale. Reality based metaphors tend to appear closer to the subject you are discussing. Fantasy based metaphors tend to be more esoteric and appear less related to the subject. The table below gives some examples.

Sample Context	Reality	Middle Ground	Fantasy
Achieving goals or targets	A person who achieved a work target.	A person who climbed a mountain	A frog who swam across a river of crocodiles.
Organisational change	An organisation that implemented a successful change.	A crew on a ship that averted disaster by changing course.	A tree who swayed in the wind, staying flexible whilst others snapped.
Dealing with a difficult person	A person who dealt with an angry member of the public.	A customer services representative who turned a complaint into a loyal customer.	A knight who turned a dragon into an ally.

You might find these metaphors in the following kinds of sources:

Reality	Middle Ground	Fantasy
• Related newspaper, magazine & research journal articles • Case studies • Personal development books • Business books	• Unrelated newspaper, magazine & journal articles • 'Chicken Soup for the Soul' type books[1]	• Aesop's fables • Fairy tales (e.g. Grimm Brothers, Hans Christian Anderson) • Children's stories (e.g. Dr Seuss, Mr. Men) • Parables and Zen koans

As a general rule of thumb, reality based metaphors appeal to the conscious mind and fantasy based metaphors appeal to the unconscious mind. If you are running corporate courses with an audience who expect you to deliver a rational, practical training session, you would be safer with the more reality based metaphors. If you are delivering a personal development workshop with some creative and/or hypnotic approaches, you might use more of the fantasy based metaphors.

iii. Using Metaphor to structure a presentation or training session
As well as using metaphor as a method of storytelling, some presenters use metaphor as a way of structuring their presentation, for example:

- Using the four seasons as a metaphor for a cyclical business process, breaking the main part of the presentation down into four key sections.
- Using the idea of running a hurdles race to achieve the gold medal, where each of the hurdles is a problem or challenge that needs to be solved to complete a project on a training course.

The Model Presenter

As a model presenter:

- Give examples to make your message more real
- Use stories and metaphors to make your point and to engage the audience
- Make sure your stories are relevant to the message and that the audience can relate to them

Chapter 10

Handling Questions

In This Chapter...

In this chapter, you will discover how to manage questions before you answer them. You will also find out the best practice steps for answering a question and will be introduced to the 'Directions of Thinking Model' which will give you a range of approaches for handling questions in any situation (including when to answer questions and when not to).

We will be exploring the following questions:

- How can you manage the types and timings of questions?
- What are the 'best practice' steps for answering questions?
- How can you invite questions?
- What is the 'Directions of Thinking Model'?
- What is 'pacing and leading' and how might you use it?
- What are some other challenges around questions and how might you handle them?

Questions and Answers

When considering questions that you might get asked, you need to think about handling the question **and** handling the answer.

With regards to handling answers, it is worth predicting questions in your preparation phase and then planning how you will reply. If you know your topic well you might not need to do this, but if the topic is contentious, be prepared for challenging questions! If the mood of a group is unsettled or you are delivering bad news, you may need to think about how you will answer difficult questions and how you might frame your answers.

Not all questions are alike in their timing, intention and relevance to your topic. So, before you answer the content of a question, you may need to decide how you will handle the question itself. Does it fit into the current flow? Will it aid understanding and learning to answer it now? Or will it distract and confuse matters to answer it now? When you are the presenter/trainer, it is up to you if, when and how you answer a question. Of course, there may be consequences to your credibility and connection if you refuse to answer *any* questions!

The first step, particularly in a presentation, is to let the audience know when you want questions, e.g. throughout, at the end or both. This sets a ground rule so the audience know what to expect and it gives you a foundation for how and when you will answer questions.

Best Practice: Steps for Taking Questions

If there was a best practice model for handling questions, it would probably be something like this... When someone asks a question, it is prudent to pay attention and listen to the questioner. If you don't hear them properly or don't understand the question, it is okay to ask them to repeat it. Play back or paraphrase the question loud enough for the whole audience to hear. This allows you to check that you understand and are about to answer the right question. It also helps the audience if they didn't hear the question themselves. If the rest of the audience didn't hear the question, they will more than likely begin to switch off. Acknowledge the question (e.g. "That's a great question") and then answer the question *to the whole audience* (rather than just the questioner). This will draw in the audience and keep them engaged. It also prevents you getting into a dialogue with the questioner which again may not be of interest to the rest of the audience. When you have answered, check that the questioner is satisfied, e.g. "does that answer your question?"

In summary...think RAC:

- Repeat the question back to the whole audience
- Answer the question to the whole audience
- Check you have answered the question

Inviting Questions: What if there are no questions?

Questions will either come spontaneously or when you create a 'space' for them. However, what if you create a space and ask the group for questions but are met with silence? If the group appears to have no questions at all, does this mean they are totally satisfied, want a break, have lost interest, think their question is stupid or don't understand the material...?

Some presenters don't get questions because their voice goes down at the end of "are there any questions" which turns it away from being an engaging request. They might also break eye contact and stare at the floor with eyebrows down as if they really don't want questions! If you want questions you need to go up towards the end of "are there any questions?" and make eye contact with eyebrows raised slightly. This creates an open expression and a psychological space for questions. Unless you don't actually want questions... then you might say "before we stop for a break, are there any questions" with voice going down at the end and eye gaze to the floor!

Another reason some groups won't ask questions or respond to your questions is that may be reflectors who need time to think; and they may feel intimidated or pressured if you are standing there waiting for them to say something. Think back to school where maybe you were daydreaming... the teacher asked a question and said your name... that's what it is like for a reflector feeling under pressure! In a training environment, we have found that when working with such a group, it is preferable to sit down and create an atmosphere of 'discussion' rather than 'teaching'.

Sometimes a group needs a kick-start to get the questions going. You can do this by saying: "Any questions?... No?... Okay, a question I am sometimes asked is-" and then answer that question. Of course, you will want to use a question that builds your credibility and connection with the group, i.e. something that you can answer easily and informatively. This will probably be something you prepared as an 'intend' or 'could' from your NIC preparation (see Chapter 5). Another way of generating a question is to refer to something an audience member might have asked you before the presentation (assuming it is a useful question and doesn't embarrass or break confidentiality), e.g. "Something Fred asked me earlier was..." or "I was asked in the coffee break..."

Handling Questions Using the 'Directions of Thinking' Model

The Directions of Thinking Model gives you various approaches to how you might respond to questions. We developed this model based on how model presenters handled questions when they were 'on the spot'.

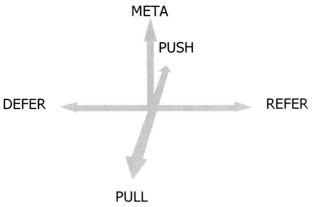

Direction	Explanation	Example Approach
Push	To push is to provide information and express your view. It is a forward motion where you are giving the audience an answer.	• Answer the question by giving information. • Suggest that they have answered the question for themselves.
Pull	To pull is to draw information from the audience. It is a slightly backward motion as you create a space for others to speak. When handling questions, this would mean asking a question back rather than immediately answering.	• Ask a question to answer the question e.g. Q: "how could you make those people redundant?" A: "how could we not? What do you imagine would happen to the business if we kept everyone?" • Ask them what they think the answer is. • Ask them questions to help them to answer their own question. • Ask for more information to help them clarify the question.
Defer	To defer is a sideways motion. You are putting off answering the question to another time (either later in the presentation/course, or to after the event). The question is 'left' unanswered for a while.	• Answer the question later when you have found out the required information. • Contain the questions to a one-to-one conversation later: "I'm happy to talk to you about that after the presentation/in the next break." • Explain that the question is outside the scope of the presentation/training.
Refer	To refer is also a sideways motion. You are taking the question to another person	• Throw the question to the group or an expert in the room for an answer.

	so they can answer it. This is where you want to make sure you get the 'right' answer.	• Give them a reference or expert where they can go to answer the question. • Tell them you will talk to an expert and then get back to them.
Meta	To 'go' meta is to step outside of or above the situation to take an alternative perspective. You might comment on the question or categorise it in some way. Or you might ask about the question or the motive behind it.	• Comment on the question (e.g. "that's a great question" or "I get this question quite a lot..."). • Categorise or label the question with a view to answering (e.g. "okay so this is a question about the process...") • Ask for their reasoning behind the question: "What makes you ask that?"

In any given situation, you might move in a couple of directions. For example, you might comment on the question initially (Meta) and then ask the group for ideas (Refer) and then complete the answer yourself (Push).

Although you can move in any direction when answering or questioning a question, answering a question tends to be primarily a push approach whereas in order to question the question, we need to step outside the question first (meta and pull). The other two directions will depend on whether you are deferring/referring the answer (still with an intention of answering it) or whether you are deferring/referring the question to somewhere/one else (and hence not answering it yourself).

'Pacing and Leading' Your Response

'Pacing and leading' is a skill that was modelled on a hypnotherapist called Milton Erickson[1]. He would join the client wherever they were psychologically and then lead them to a more healthy and productive state of mind. 'Pacing' means matching the audience, starting from where they are but with a view to 'leading' i.e. moving them to another perspective. The beauty of pacing and leading is that you are not disagreeing with the audience, even though you then move to a position that would have been untenable if you had simply started there.

Sometimes a presenter is put in an awkward situation of being asked to take sides. This is particularly true in times of having to deliver bad news (e.g. change in an organisation leading to relocation or redundancies). The audience mentality takes the position of: "you are with us or against us".

A Case In Point

Imagine you are delivering the news to your team that the office will be relocating some distance away and so the team will either have to move with the company or leave. An angry member of the team says to you: "This change affects you as well, what do you think? How do you feel about it?"

The question asked in the box above could create a double bind for the presenter. If they take the view that the change is okay, then they may be perceived as a 'management puppet' (and hence lose connection with the group). If they take the team's side that the change is bad, then they are not representing the organisation or delivering their message and so they may lose credibility. The trick here is to walk the fine line from one to the other: "When I first heard about the change I had some of the same questions and concerns that you have been raising, but now I have had time to think it through, I can see why the business needs to make the change and I am focussing on how we make the best of it and make it work for us going forwards."

This kind of approach suggests that you have had a progression in your thinking, moving from one place to another. You are empathising with both sides and suggesting to the team that once *they* have thought about it, they can join you in trying to make the best of it.

Other Challenges When Handling Questions

Here are some other frequently asked questions about handling questions with some bullet point ideas on what to do:

a) What if someone asks a question and you don't know the answer?

- If it is a case of not really understanding what is being asked, you could ask them to rephrase the question.
- Often, the best bet here is to admit that you don't know but that you will find out and come back to them.
- If there is someone in the audience (or the panel) that may have the expertise, you could refer to them. Alternatively you could check with the audience?

b) What if the questioner is quiet or I can't understand his accent?

- Apologise for not being able to hear them and ask them to repeat the question.
- If you still didn't get it, take responsibility for not hearing them (rather than blame them) and ask them to say the question louder or to slow down.
- If you still don't get it, you could blame the acoustics in the room and let them know that you will catch up with them afterwards to answer their question. Often by this stage, someone with a clearer voice nearby them will repeat the

question to you. If they don't it may imply that no-one can hear/understand them.

c) What if the questioner wants to engage in a dialogue?

- The problem here is that when only one person is asking questions, the rest of the audience begins to switch off. Hence, it is important to answer the whole audience in order to keep them engaged.
- If the same person asks more questions, you might say: "I get that you have a lot of questions, so I'll catch up with you afterwards and we can discuss them."
- If they won't let it go, tell them (politely!) that others may have questions. You might say, looking to the rest of the audience: "Does anyone else, aside from John, have any questions?"

d) What if someone makes statements instead of asking questions?

- You can treat it as a question and respond to it, adding or putting forward your perspective on the topic or on what they have said specifically.
- If someone makes a statement during the questions phase, you might say (politely): "Okay, thank you." And then to the group "Are there any questions?"
- You might ask inquisitively: "Is there a question there?"

For more ideas on handling difficult behaviours and situations, see Chapter 11.

Model Making

As a model presenter:

- Develop different approaches for handling awkward questions
- Prepare your topic so that you are ready for questions
- Repeat, Answer and Check when someone asks you a question

The Model Presenter

Chapter 11

Managing Difficulties

In This Chapter...

In this chapter, you will learn about a range of difficulties a presenter/trainer might face and how to prevent or deal with these situations. The presenter will sometimes create their own problems or they may be faced with things they have no apparent control over, for example difficult messages, environments and audience behaviours. Here you will be given some ideas on how to handle each of them with a view to giving you more confidence when presenting.

We will be exploring the following questions:

- How do presenters sometimes create their own difficulties?
- What are some of the difficulties a presenter might face and how can they be handled?

Yes, but what if...?

One of the reasons some presenters and trainers get nervous is that they are concerned about the 'what if's. For example, what if the audience members misbehave, what if the power point doesn't work, what if the audience finds me boring... what if I embarrass myself?

We will be dealing with nerves directly in the next chapter, but here we are looking at hints and tips on how to avoid difficulties and how to handle them if they do happen.

The Model Presenter

When Presenters Create their Own Difficulties

How (and why) might a presenter create their own difficulties? Given that presenting can be challenging enough already, it would be unusual for a presenter to create problems on purpose, so what are some of the things they might do which could create a problematic environment and audience?

Making Mistakes

Mistakes may be down to poor planning, an oversight in proofreading or some incorrect or missing knowledge. If you realise that there is a mistake in your slides or handout, usually the best approach is to pick it up, apologise, tell the audience the correct information and then move on. An audience will have a tolerance for the occasional spelling mistake or incorrect figure, so owning it and putting it right is probably the best bet. If you have rapport with the group, you might make a quick joke of it. Sometimes spelling mistakes can produce amusingly unexpected meanings.

> A Case In Point
>
> I once had a line in a self-assessment questionnaire which should have read: "Sometimes I spread myself too thinly" but for some reason the copier had stretched the page and I hadn't checked it... it now read: "Sometimes I spread myself". Fortunately I had strong rapport with the group and there was plenty of laughter and a useful story to refer to later.

If the mistake is a case of incorrect or missing knowledge, the only way you will know that is when someone in the audience wants to argue with you. Unless you absolutely need to, our experience is that it is best not to take a position on what you said (i.e. avoid getting into an argument about it). If someone is telling you that alternative information is correct and you are not sure, say you'll find out. If you are absolutely sure, tell the person that you are sure your information is correct but that you are happy to check it. If you find that you are right (and if necessary if you were wrong), let the audience know the correct information when you have checked. Of course, there may be times you have a self-proclaimed expert in the room and you may choose to handle this in other ways. The 'know it all' is covered later in this chapter.

Making 'Absolute' Statements

A presenter/trainer is likely to run into trouble from time if they insist on generalising and acting as if their view is the 'only' truth, for example:

- Absolute statements including words like like: *always/never/all/no-one/everyone* may invite a member of the audience to disagree by citing an exception or stating that it not their experience.
- When a presenter says that things *can't* happen or that they *should/shouldn't*, they may find someone in the audience disagreeing and citing a counter example.
- By saying that 'X causes Y' (e.g. 'increased prices causes a loss of customers') or X is the same as Y (e.g. 'eating meat is the same as murdering a person'), there may again be someone who disagrees and has a counter position.

These are just examples and it may be challenging for a presenter to avoid 'absolute statements' altogether. However, if the presenter tempers their language with qualifiers like 'most people', 'usually' and 'often', the audience will find it hard to argue. In this sense, we are being 'artfully vague' as Milton Erickson[1] would have it. The same is true of avoiding phrases like: "It has been proven that" when "it could be argued" or "the evidence suggests that" is less open to resistance.

If you find you have fallen foul of an absolute statement and someone wants to argue with you, you might ask them to hold their argument until later in the proceedings.

Whilst running a course a few years ago, I spoke of the importance of emotions in the workplace. One of the participants insisted that emotions were not important and should play no part in the workplace. He seemed to be advocating the 'leave your emotions at home' philosophy. I confess to being somewhat nonplussed at first, but I asked him to hold the thought and that we'd revisit it towards the end of the course. At the end of the course I asked for key learning points and fortunately (from my perspective) he reported that he had changed his mind!

Presenter Behaviours

As discussed previously elsewhere, a presenter might create problems for themselves in the way they deliver the presentation; for example, in their voice (e.g. too fast/slow, too quiet/loud, monotone) or body language (e.g. dancing, hands in pockets, back to the audience) or language (e.g. as above) or content level (e.g. too detailed/lightweight). If a presenter makes no effort to 'close the gap' and engage the audience, the group will likely switch off and become distracted.

A presenter is not necessarily responsible for every presentation problem but they need to look at what they are doing or not doing that may be causing or perpetuating a difficult situation.

'External' Difficulties

The main 'external' difficulties (i.e. those apparently not directly caused by the presenter) are likely to fall into one or more of three main categories:

o Difficult Content/Message
o Difficult Environment
o Difficult People/Behaviours

1) Difficult Content/Message

a. Bad or Controversial News

If your message is controversial or you know the mood of the group is going to be less than positive, you would be wise to set time aside for comments and questions at the start (or just after you have delivered your difficult message). If there are too many to handle easily, write them down on a flipchart or white board and respond to them once they are written down. This approach is covered in more detail later in the chapter.

b. Someone else's material

The problem with other people's material is that it is not yours! It didn't come from your mind and hence may be challenging to get you 'head around'. What if the material is a bit dull? Do you have to follow their script word for word? If you have to deliver someone else's material, it is worth finding out how much you can alter and adapt. Even if you have to use their slides or manuals it is still about putting things into your own words, hence 'lighting up' your own neurology. When using power-point slides, it is important not to just say what is on the screen. You need to explain it in your own way. If you are reading what is on the slide, what is the point of you being there... or of the material being delivered in presentation format when the audience could have read it via an email?

A Case In Point

In my early days of training, I sometimes worked as a subcontractor. This meant using not just other people's materials, but also working to their 'script'. The script had obviously been written for non-trainers as it said things like: "Tell the group this story and then pause for laughter"!

The Model Presenter

Talking through black and white data can be tedious. As discussed in Chapter 9, you need to put in your own personal examples, stories and anecdotes to bring the material alive with experiences the audience can relate to.

2. Difficult Environment

a. Over-running

If you are presenting as part of an event, i.e. there are people speaking before and perhaps after you, there may be times when you end up with less time than you expected. Either the event itself is running late, or the person introducing you takes longer than anticipated, or a previous speaker takes up more time than they officially had allocated. These things will tend to be outside of your control. When you get to speak, you will either have to condense what you had to say, or perpetuate the overrun. If you have been told to take your allocated time and that the organisers will make the time up elsewhere then fine – they have made that choice for you.

Of course, the 'right' choice will depend on the situation. Sometimes you might be delighted that you have only fifteen minutes instead of half an hour! If you are going to take your full time, it is good to let the organisers know that this is your intention. It is up to them to reorganise the event schedule.

To condense what you are presenting, go back to the NIC (Need-Intend-Could) System (as discussed in chapter 5). If you have prepared yourself well, you will know what the 'Needs' (i.e. the most important bits of information) are. You might let the audience know that more information is available afterwards (e.g. through conversation, email, website or printed material).

You could get creative and say: "I have less time than I was anticipating so in order to make sure I give you the specific information you need, how about we go straight to questions and answers?" Obviously this will only work if the audience already have some knowledge about your topic or actually want to know more.

b. Technical issues

The simple answer to this is: find out who the technical support person is before hand or take a technical person with you. It is better to have someone else fiddling with crashing computers instead of the audience impatiently watching you. Then you can carry on with the presentation whilst the issue gets fixed.

c. Location issues

Chapter 3 makes some suggestions for a model environment but things can sometimes be less than ideal. Of course, location issues can sometimes be avoided by putting in a specific request for what you need (e.g. "I'd like a quiet room that can comfortably take 12 people sitting in a U-shape with tables. It would be useful to have somewhere nearby that we can break out to – a coffee area would be fine.")

Make sure everyone (including you) has clear directions and protocols (e.g. where to park, where to report into).

However, you often have to go with what you are given! One of the most disarming ways of handling location issues is using a degree of light-heartedness. If you have done everything you can to prevent and cure any issues, then light-heartedness will keep *you* from getting frustrated, and then hopefully the audience too. The spirit to capture is: 'we are all in this together'. In terms of light humour, here are a couple of examples:

- Comment on the situation: If the room is too small, you might comment that it will be cosy, but at least we will get to know each other by the end of the day (then use a breakout area as much as possible). If you are in a glass walled training room and people are looking in as they walk by, you might make reference to discovering what it feels like to live in a zoo! The important thing is that you are teasing and not being sarcastic or vindictive (especially if you are at a client's venue!)

- If you suspect an issue may occur, you can 'preframe' it, i.e. mention it before it happens.

A Case In Point

I was at a venue where I guessed there would be the noise of hammers and drills (due to some renovation work), so I mentioned in my introduction that I was getting a bit paranoid as recently it seemed I was being followed by a man with a hammer and a drill. The idea here is that if the noise starts later, the audience will have a different interpretation. Instead of getting irritated, they were more likely to tease me that the man is after me again! If not, I could bring it up myself: "Did I just imagine that... or is the man with the hammer back?" By associating the noise with humour, the noise becomes funny.

3. Difficult Audience Behaviour

This section covers what perhaps most presenters fear... the difficult person or difficult group. Here we will explore a range of challenging behaviours with some ideas on how to handle them.

Before we get on to some specific examples, here are some general ideas on dealing with challenging behaviours:

- Treat the person with respect and endeavour to maintain their self esteem.

- Thank them for introducing issues. Sincerely value their input.
- Remember a 'difficult person' may be a person having difficulty understanding 'what', 'why' or 'how'.
- Remain friendly, open and honest. Seek to maintain rapport with the person even if you need to change their behaviour.
- If possible and necessary, elicit support from the rest of the audience.

With these general tips in mind, here are some specific examples:

a. Know it all (& think they know it all!)

The 'know it all' usually wants to play the expert. At worst they want to play one-upmanship with you and at best they seem to want to be acknowledged for their knowledge and cleverness. Of course, there is also the 'think they know it all' who may not necessarily be correct but will act the same way as the 'know it all'. The 'know it all' will usually act in a 'push' manner, so using the Directions of Thinking Model (see chapter 10), here are 5 different 'directions' you could take to handle this type of behaviour:

Push	Hold your ground. Only do this if you are absolutely sure of your facts and have hard evidence to back it up. Be prepared for them to argue back and if this is the case, change direction (e.g. meta, defer or refer).
Pull	Ask them: "how do you know that?" Ask for more information: "tell me more about what you are saying." If appropriate, acknowledge their knowledge and/or change direction (e.g. meta, defer or refer)
Defer	Tell them you are happy to discuss it further but for the sake of time, you will discuss it with them afterwards.
Refer	Reference literature or recent research or a 'greater authority' (e.g. the CEO/MD). Take it higher than yourself in giving 'evidence' of what an expert's expert has said.
Meta	Comment on the situation. E.g. "It seems we have a difference of perspectives and no way of proving it either way here and now." Then defer to later.

The Model Presenter

b. Personal agenda

Sometimes you might get someone who has a different agenda to that which you are presenting. They might not want to be there or they may want to deviate to their own cause and will try to use your presentation/course as a platform to make their case. They are trying to *push*. If you have an individual who obviously has their own agenda, the best way to handle it is to *defer* - tell them you are happy to discuss it afterwards on a one-to-one basis. If they carry on or come back to it later, repeat that you are happy to discuss it afterwards. If they are alone in their cause, the audience may get fed up with them. As long as you are being seen to handle it (or attempt to handle it) the audience will usually support you.

In some public forums, where individuals may have an 'axe to grind', the organisers of the presentation will sometimes hand out forms with space to write questions and issues that are collected in at the end of the presentation. The group are told that any questions or issues they raise will be addressed within a certain time period. If someone raises an issue that is outside the scope of the meeting or presentation, they are reminded to put the question/issue onto the form to be handed in.

If the *group* has an alternative agenda (or agendas) to you, you may have to *pull*. This may be a case where the audience will not let you get on with your own presentation. You cannot push because they will continually try to draw you away to their issues. Rather than feel pressured or 'on the back foot', you need to take control of the proceedings by 'capturing issues'. Use a flipchart or whiteboard to write down the issues being presented by individuals in the group. This is one of those situations where you need to be able to write sideways on the board/chart so that you can keep eye-contact with the group – if you turn your back on them you may lose control. Because you are writing, they now have to go at your pace and go one at a time. In addition, as you write, most people will moderate their language and think about what they want to say as it is being 'published'. Most people seem happy to 'queue' if you are handling the group's issues. They are more likely to wait their turn rather than insist their issue is more important than another member of the group. When you have all the issues you can use this as an agenda and answer them in the order of your choosing.

c. Doodling

If someone is doodling, let them. It will help to prevent them from daydreaming. Many people doodle to help them concentrate on listening[2].

d. Side talking

If there is a momentary exchange between two people, you might choose to let it go. However, if it goes on (and if it is loud enough to be distracting) whilst you are talking, an 'adult' approach is to ask to them: "Is everything okay?" The usual response is: 'sorry' and they stop. Alternatively, it gives them a chance to voice something if necessary. If there is a side conversation happening when someone else from the group is talking, you might say to them: "Let's stick together here... Roger (the original speaker), you were saying..."

e. Quiet/deadpan

A quiet group may mean they don't want to be there or it may be you have a group of reflectors who are shy or naturally quiet. The key is in the body language, particularly the faces. Do they seem as if they are quietly attentive or do they seem to be quietly angry, 'seething' and/or contemptuous?

A quietly attentive group will often respond better if you sit down and talk with them rather than stand and behave in an extrovert fashion. Match the mood of the group and they may begin to come out of their collective shell. If necessary, get them into small discussion groups.

Depending on how much time you have, a quietly angry group may need to be 'processed'. If you are only there for a few minutes, focus on delivering your message. If you need to work with the emotion of the group however, see the ideas above on how to handle a group with their own agenda.

f. The Rebel

The rebel is usually a 'mis-matcher' who wants to find a way of disagreeing with you, perhaps by supplying a counter example of what you are saying. If possible find a higher level at which to agree with them, or acknowledge there are situations where what they say may be true.

By using 'possibility' language (see Chapter 8), it becomes harder for people to disagree with you. If you say: "people don't like rudeness", a rebel can disagree and give examples of people who love rudeness. If you say: "most people don't like rudeness", the rebel cannot directly disagree. If they give examples of people who love rudeness, they have not actually disagreed with you! If they want to argue with the word 'most' they are still accepting that 'people don't like rudeness', it is just a matter of how many people!

If the rebel is mismatching on a behavioural level (e.g. not joining in with activities), where possible make the behaviour okay. If it is not too disruptive, give them permission e.g. not to join in activities). The point behind this is that if it their rebellion is made okay, it is no longer rewarding. Sometimes, you can label their behaviour and give them a 'role'. This needs to be done with rapport and with a twinkle in your eye! For example:

- The critical perfectionist who points out spelling mistakes becomes a 'spellchecker'
- The negative one who can only see what is wrong with things becomes 'devil's advocate'
- The pragmatist who tells you things won't work becomes the 'reality checker'
- The 'mis-matcher' becomes the 'counter example provider'.

A Case In Point

Whilst running a team development event, one individual participated in the first activity but didn't want to do things the way the rest of the team did. Eventually they persuaded him to take part in their solution. It was all good humoured and it seemed that he was being playful. The second activity involved writing ideas on flip chart and the team was split into subgroups. His group had a few 'irreverent' ideas compared to the other teams. The person reporting back said that the unusual ideas were from 'Fred', but that was "just like him". This was also said in good spirit however, I was beginning to feel an edge! Fred appeared to be very pragmatic and was a little aloof and unsmiling. At this point I said that the ability to think and act differently was a hugely important part of innovation and even though the manager (who was there) may sometimes find it challenging, if no-one shook the status quo from time to time there would be nothing new and improved. In effect, I was making his behaviour okay and indirectly encouraging him to do it more. At this point he cheered up immensely and participated fully, helping his teammates for the rest of the day.

Worst Case Scenarios

If you are dealing with a more extreme or unwanted behaviour, here are some final tips:

The Model Presenter

1) Ground-ruling

Set up some ground-rules at the beginning of the session. For example, if there is a growing culture of people answering mobile phones in presentations and courses, ask people to switch their phone off or put their phone on silent. You might also add: "If you are in a position where you might need to take an urgent call, please take it outside."

If someone begins doing something on the event which is disruptive, you can set a ground-rule there and then, e.g. if someone is verbally unpleasant to someone else: "I'm happy with some good natured banter, but that crosses a line. I'm going to ask you to hold back from saying things like that because you are on the edge of bullying."

2) Disagreeing

We tend to make it a principle not to overtly disagree with a member of the audience because to do so sets up a conflicting position. If there is a way of using reframing (e.g. "I wonder... if you went and did that at work... what impact that might have on your career") or humour (e.g. "Woah... easy tiger!"), we will use that to defuse the situation and move on. Perhaps we might then talk to that person at a break time.

However, if someone genuinely suggests something illegal or immoral or is acting with prejudice or discrimination, it may be time to directly disagree. Even then, we will disagree not with the person themselves but with what they are saying (e.g. "to do that would be illegal").

3) Asking someone to leave

If worst comes to worst and someone is continually disruptive (despite the ideas above), you might have to ask them to leave. This will depend on your circumstances as to how easy this is (e.g. whether you are internal/external, senior/junior and whether you have explicit/implied permission). Perhaps the best approach is to call a time out/break and speak to them on a one to one basis (so they don't have an audience of their own to act out the drama). If you cannot take a break, you might have to appeal to the group to help you, although this is perhaps a last resort!

Final Words

If you are prepared for difficulties and have strategies in place to handle them, you will find yourself, with experience, getting less and less difficult people in your audiences.

As long as you are physically safe, treat any difficult person as a challenge and an opportunity to expand your own 'map of the world'. For every challenge you handle, you will gain more strategies. As you gain more strategies you will have more choices and hence you will become more flexible and resilient.

Model Making

As a model presenter:

- Take responsibility for you own part in any miscommunications and misunderstandings
- Have some back-up plans... prepare to prevent and resolve difficult situations
- Learn a range of strategies for dealing with unhelpful behaviours from the audience

The Model Presenter

Chapter 12

Managing Nerves and Fear: Connecting to Confidence

In This Chapter...

In this chapter, you will be introduced to the comforting concept of 'Audience Tolerance' and uncover why some people get nervous about presenting. We will then cover a range of ideas to help handle nerves.

We will be exploring the following questions:

- What is 'Audience Tolerance' and how does this help you?
- Why do people get nervous at the idea of presenting?
- What can you do to feel more calm and confident?

Audience Tolerance

When running presentation skills courses, group participants often report feeling very nervous about (and when doing) the first presentation. So, when they have completed their presentation, we ask them: "On a scale of 1-10 (where 10 is high) how nervous did you feel?" This gives the presenter an opportunity to quantify how they felt. Depending on their internal experience and confidence levels, most often, the response is somewhere between 7 and 10 (with some people saying more than 10)! However, if someone scores themselves as highly nervous, we then ask the audience: "On a scale of 1-10 (where 10 is high), how nervous did they appear?" The answer is usually about 2 or 5. Ironically, the audience often add that the speaker seemed really confident. Whilst this may create a sense of confusion for the speaker (who will do their best to deflect the feedback), it is none-the-less useful information.

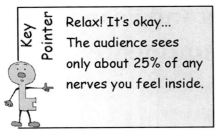

Key Pointer

Relax! It's okay... The audience sees only about 25% of any nerves you feel inside.

It seems that what the audience sees is only about 25% of how you, as the speaker, feel. We believe it is essential for every presenter to understand this point. If, as a speaker, we perceive that the audience is noticing everything we feel, we will feel more vulnerable than we need to (and then go through a vicious circle of nervousness). If we know that the audience has a high level of tolerance for our nervousness, it ceases to become such an issue. This can help to break the circular nature of nerves.

Whilst it is possible that the audience may pick up on exaggerated nervous behaviour, they are usually trying to focus on the content of the presentation/training. Most of the behaviour is filtered out (at least consciously).

The other thing to consider is that most audiences *want you to succeed*. This may be because they like you but it may also be that they don't want to have to feel uncomfortable or embarrassed by a poor presenter! When you are in the audience, unless you have an unsupportive agenda, you want the presenter to be engaging, informative and entertaining. Most audience members will be sitting there glad that it is you up the front and not them!

Nervousness: What and why?

When standing up and speaking to a group of people, the presenter becomes the centre of attention... all eyes are on them. They are, in effect, performing. The audience has an expectation of them to perform well, and they may have expectations of themselves. This can lead to an experience of not only pressure, but also vulnerability. There is no-where to hide!

Presentation nerves are common amongst those for whom presenting is not their day job. What is interesting about nervousness is that it is one of those emotions that appear to get refuelled. Normally, an emotion comes and goes, perhaps lasting ninety seconds or so (according to Jill Bolte-Taylor[1]). However, nervousness seems to loop in some way, so that we continue to feel it. This may be because we end up feeling nervous about feeling nervous and so we create what is called a 'meta-state' of nervousness (see Michael Hall[2]), which perpetuates the unresourceful experience. We can even feel nervous thinking about or imagining a presentation that we are *not at that point delivering*, which suggests that it is not the actual presentation we fear but perhaps the idea of it!

Although most of us are familiar with nervousness (which is similar to the experience of anxiety and fear), here are some of the typical internal symptoms:

Physiological	Mental
Heart rate increase	Mind goes blank (aka 'drying')
Butterflies in the stomach	Negative internal dialogue
Dry mouth	Feeling disassociated
Reddening/blushing	Can't focus
Breathless	

These symptoms are known as the 'fight/flight' reaction where the body is getting ready to do battle or run away. The heart rate increases as adrenaline kicks in and more blood is diverted from the stomach and head and into the major muscles. In a perceived environment of immediate risk, the body doesn't want the conscious

mind thinking too much. In this sense, the unconscious mind takes over and acts on autopilot and it is this unconscious reaction that makes nervousness a tough problem for some people to overcome.

In terms of external symptoms of nervousness, the unconscious mind appears to have a range of behaviours, all of which seem to fit the 'fight/flight' model. Here are some of those unconscious behaviours:

- *Dancing, pacing and rocking*: this behaviour can appear as if the presenter:
  o is trying to comfort themselves,
  o is unsteady on their feet,
  o can't make their mind up where to stand or
  o needs to go to the toilet!
- *Disfluencies*: this behaviour is where someone adds noises and words into the middle of their speech. It can appear as if the presenter:
  o is uncomfortable with gaps,
  o is unsure of what they are saying or
  o has lost control of their speech system.
  Examples are:
  o Pronounced 'um's and 'ah's
  o Repetitive words (also known as 'verbal fillers') e.g. 'like', 'sort of', 'you know', 'right', 'kind of'.
- *Blushing*
- *Talking quickly*
- *Nervous laughter*
- *Repetitive cough, sniff, clearing throat ('ahem'!)*

At best, the audience won't notice these unconscious behaviours; however at worst, these behavioural symptoms may have an impact on the speaker's credibility. If, as an audience member, you become aware of a speaker's repetitive behaviour, it can become hard not to focus on it and then, of course, you are probably not listening to the message.

Why do we get nervous and have strange nervous automatic behaviours? If our unconscious behaviour has the potential to be counterproductive, why do we do it? What might be the 'positive intention' of the unconscious mind in this context (i.e. what positive things might the behaviour give us)? The primary 'positive intention' is usually protection (i.e. to survive) and so it is likely that the unconscious is trying to get us out of there! As well as this primary level of protection, we may then build a more conscious secondary layer. If we begin to fear presenting, this gives us an excuse not to have to do it. We are less likely to put ourselves in the frame for presenting if we know we might have the unconscious counterproductive symptoms (e.g. pacing, blushing etc).

If the 'positive intention' of the unconscious in this context is protection and safety, how might we build this into a strategy for presenting? One of the useful things about fear is that it may make us want to prepare ourselves. A helpful exercise in preparing for a presentation is asking yourself: "what could go wrong?" with a view to contingency planning. For each thing that could go wrong, ask yourself: "How could I prevent that from happening or deal with it if it does?" Consider things like equipment failure, no-shows, more people than expected, awkward behaviour and time being 'cut short'. Also consider what questions you might get asked and how you will answer or deal with them. If in doubt, have a read through some of the previous chapters of this book, which is designed to address all of these issues!

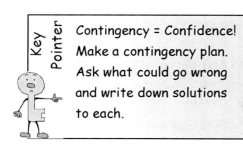

Key Pointer

Contingency = Confidence!
Make a contingency plan.
Ask what could go wrong and write down solutions to each.

When we have our content clearly structured and contingency plans in place, we cannot help but feel more confident. We now know that worst case scenarios are catered for and at the very least we can deliver a message to the audience. And if you really want to eliminate concerns about nerves, the next part of the chapter will give you plenty of ideas.

Handling Nerves: Solutions and Ideas

Throughout this book, we have used the concept of 'closing the gap' between yourself and the audience. We believe that the primary point of calm and confidence evolves when you feel that you are *part of the group* (rather than a presenter separate from the audience).

In this section, we are looking at a range of ideas and solutions to overcoming nervousness with a view to developing feelings of calm and confidence. Remember that different things work for different people. We have categorised the ideas as follows:

1. Change your focus
2. Change your perspective
3. Change your self-awareness
4. Change your behaviour
5. Change the situation

1. Change your focus

a) Focus on your desired state... How do you want to feel?

First things first, if you don't want to feel nervous or anxious, how do you want to feel instead? When people focus on their 'problem' state, e.g. nervousness, guess what they get! The same applies if they tell themselves that they don't want to feel nervous. What else can the brain do but focus on 'nervous'. The brain doesn't really work so well with negative commands like this. In one sense, it
acts like a search engine, so what you request will come back in the form of associations and memories. So, when you are *not* feeling

nervous or anxious, what *will* you be feeling... e.g. confident, calm, excited, ready, strong? By focussing on: "I want to feel confident", you will generate a completely different neurology and hence physiology.

b) Focus on outcomes

Remember the purpose of your presentation. Focus on what you want the audience to know or do as a result of the presentation. How will your presentation benefit the audience and/or the organisation... what will they gain?

c) Focus on 'closing the gap'

Focus on the audience and make connections. Make eye contact and talk with people. Use the ideas in Chapter 2 on engaging the mind of the audience and closing the gap between yourself and the audience.

2. Change your perspective

Nervousness is an interesting state in that it is very close, if not the other side of the coin, to excitement. If you thought you were feeling nervous, how would it be to know that you are actually feeling excited about doing the presentation! The main difference between nervousness and excitement is the label we attach to it. Even if we can't initially control the physical sensations, we *can* control what we call it.

A Case In Point	Whenever I feel a flutter in my stomach and my heart rate increases before an event, I know I am feeling excited. Just to play, I even tell myself that I'm feeling 'jazzed' or 'pumped' because those words make me smile... and more motivated! Emotions are a form of energy... so utilise them!

Another way of looking at it is: *at least you are feeling something*! When someone tells us they get nervous, we see this as a good sign because it means the presentation is important to them. They want to get it right and do a good job and we admire that. Nervousness encourages people to prepare and plan what they are going to say. If we were about to do a big event and we weren't feeling a little 'fluttery', we'd be concerned that we were being blasé!

And by the way, if you are worried about a few 'um's and 'ah's in your speech, it is likely that a tolerable amount of 'disfluency' is actually useful for the listener as it gives them more time to process what you are saying[3].

3. Change your self-awareness

When we present and train, we experience ourselves from the 'inside'. From this perspective we cannot really see or hear how we are doing, we can only *feel*. In this instance, our feelings are not always the best indicator since whatever emotion we are experiencing, any feedback we receive will be filtered through those emotions. The problem here is that emotions tend to act like lenses, distorting what is going on inside and around us.

Imagine someone on a presentation skills course. After delivering their presentation, they are given feedback from members of the audience. Depending on their feelings and beliefs about themselves, unless they possess a significant degree of self awareness and receptiveness, they are likely to 'edit' the feedback according to their own 'map of the world'. If they are self-deprecating, they are likely to filter out the positive feedback and will focus on anything they think they did wrong.

So here is the best advice that you may (or may not) find challenging to accept! The most effective feedback you will ever receive is seeing and hearing yourself. By recording yourself presenting/training you will gain an observer perspective that is an invaluable tool in developing, improving and hence building confidence.

So let us get beyond the initial reaction to being recorded. When we video delegates on courses many react initially as if we had just taken a gun out of our bag and aimed it at them! Second reaction: "Oh no, I hate seeing myself and hearing my voice!" Third reaction (after being recorded): "Is that really me? Do I sound like that?" However, having got past the 'shock and denial' stages, most people begin to experience the value in seeing and hearing themselves presenting.

Instead of feeling embarrassed, how would you *like* to feel about seeing and hearing yourself? Would you like to feel neutral, comfortable and/or perhaps curious? We encourage you to go further than this and get *really fascinated* about who you are, how you look, how you sound and how you behave. This is how you have created yourself in this life time! Assuming they are not ruining credibility or connection, celebrate your quirks and unique characteristics. Be proud of your accent... it is part of your heritage, culture and upbringing. Let your uniqueness be your strength. It is okay to enjoy your strengths as well as choosing to get flexible with behaviours you want to change or develop. The way through embarrassment and self-consciousness is to get used to yourself!

Record yourself from time to time (both video and audio) and watch/listen to it. Get familiar with how you look and sound so it ceases to become unusual or weird. When you are ready to use video/audio recorded feedback to develop your skills as a presenter, you might want to take a note of the following, particularly in terms of what works well and what works less well:

a) What do you do naturally and automatically?
b) What are some of your unconscious behaviours? For example, those described earlier in this chapter:
- Dancing, pacing and rocking

- Disfluencies: Pronounced 'Um's and 'Ah's, Repetitive words (also known as 'verbal fillers') e.g. like, sort of, you know, right, kind of.
- Blushing
- Talking quickly
- Nervous laughter

c)   How much variation is there in your voice? Are you a little 'monotone' (monotonous) or do you vary your volume and pace and pitch?

d)   What language do you use? (See chapter 8 for more details.)

- What sensory language do you use? Do you use the full range?
- How are your positive/negative instructions? Are you purposeful with the images you create in the mind of the audience? Is your language positive and outcome focussed most of the time?

By becoming more aware of your own behaviours from an external observer perspective, you are more likely to interpret your internal feeling more accurately. You then have a better chance of interrupting unwanted patterns (as long as you know what you want to replace them with). You can also appreciate those things that work well and that look, sound and feel good.

4. Change Your Behaviour

A change of behaviour might be to simply change your posture. For example, how do you stand when you are confident? For most people, the posture of confidence means both feet planted firmly on the ground. Also, notice the inch difference in your breastbone between down ('collapsed'/slumped) and up (confident/shoulders back). Notice what happens when you stand 'strong' with your shoulders back... and when you are doing this, feel what it is like to say to yourself: "Come on... bring it on!"

A change of behaviour might be to practice, i.e. to get familiar with your material by running through it. Alternatively, it may mean taking every opportunity to get in front of an audience or even to speak up in groups (e.g. meetings). When we practice, we reduce the unconscious mind's perception of threat. Standing and speaking in front of an audience then becomes more comfortable to a point where it moves on to being rewarding and enjoyable.

Some unconscious behaviours might seem harder to change, for example the disfluencies ('um's and 'ar's), talking too quickly or blushing. If conscious intervention or practice hasn't helped, you might want to try something that appears on the surface absolutely nuts, but is amazingly successful. This surprising approach is paradoxical in nature and is known as 'prescribing the symptom'. For example:

- if someone speaks too quickly, we encourage them to purposefully speed up,
- if someone uses a lot of 'ums' or 'you know', we encourage them to add more,
- if someone blushes, we ask them to blush more,
- if someone unconsciously dances, we ask them to dance even more.

The point with this type of 'paradoxical intervention' is that the person is taking control of the seemingly uncontrollable 'symptom', but instead of resisting it, they are going with it and exaggerating it. Not only does this make it conscious, it also makes it seem silly (to the person it affects). Adding the humour element creates a degree of acceptance and so the symptom seems to disappear (or reduce dramatically). As a note, if you are using this approach to help someone else, make sure you have a high degree of rapport with them and they know they are doing this for their best interest (rather than for you to have a laugh at their expense).

5) Change the Situation

a) Own the Room

Part of feeling confident is to own the space you are presenting/training in. It is your show and your room. When you are at the front, you are in charge of the content and the process, so take a moment to remind yourself: "This is mine. This is my domain!"

b) Contingency Plan

When preparing, draw up a list of things that could go wrong and come up with three or more solutions for each item on the list. Check these ideas out with others. Get other people's input as to how they deal with situations (particularly the presenters and trainers you admire). Give yourself options so if any of these things happen, you are ready from them.

c) Handle the 'mind Blank'

One of the greatest fears of any presenter is the 'mind blank' (or as actors call it 'drying'!) Here's the secret... there may be no perfect solution for *avoiding* the mind blank (because even if we are well rehearsed and confident, it can happen if we are distracted or interrupted). It will most likely have happened to everyone at some stage, even the best speakers and actors, so you are in great company!

Fortunately, for most presenters and trainers, it is okay to have some notes or power point slides to refer to and use as a memory jogger. Prepare well, with a good structure and you can come back to that structure. One great trick is to use a handout which you give out at the start or put on chairs before the event. You have a copy of the handout too and you have your notes written in the relevant places in the handout. During the session you can refer people to the handout, e.g. "Have a look at page 3 for a moment" and then your notes are there! Now, everyone is looking at the handout, including you (so there is group rapport). They are not focussed on you for the moment, so you can use your hidden notes to work from. As an aside, handouts are great for controlling the audience too because you can shift their attention to or away from it at any time (e.g. "Just putting the handout to one side for the time being...")

Give yourself at least three strategies for handling the mind blank in case it ever happens, for example:

- *Use humour*: This can help maintain connection with the audience while you get your mind back in action. For example: "I have no idea where we are at this point... who am I again?" If it is more important to maintain credibility, use another technique.
- *Ask the audience*: If you have rapport and credibility is already built, you can ask the audience e.g. "where are we up to?" or "what was the last point made there?"
- *Have a quick anecdote ready*: "You know, when I was at school, sometimes a teacher would ask me what they had just said... I thought it was to test whether I'd been listening or not... now I realise they had forgotten where they were up to... I'd have a made a great teacher! Now... what was I just talking about before I interrupted myself?"
- *And have another anecdote ready*: "Have you ever had your mind go blank... actors call it 'drying'. Apparently Ian Holm had a period of time in his career where he 'dried'... so I guess I'm in good company!"
- *Be honest*: "Oh dear, my mind has just gone blank. Let me just check the next point." Then check your notes.
- *Use the handout*: Direct the audience to your handout whilst you reconnect with your material.
- *Ask for questions*: "Okay... so are there any questions at this point?" This may give you a moment to check your notes,

look at the power point or simply remember where you are in your structure.

Model Making

As a model presenter:

- Put any nervousness into perspective
- Remember that the audience only see about 25% of what you feel inside
- Give yourself confidence by having contingency plans for handling what could go wrong
- Focus on how you want to feel... confident... calm... ready!

Appendix 1: The Modelling Project

Modelling

Modelling is a term used in NLP (Neuro-Linguistic Programming) and could be defined as: *'a methodology for establishing how people do excellence in a particular context'*. The context for this book is 'communicating and working with an audience'.

Although we have a strong background in NLP, we are not tied to the field. In fact, we consider NLP to be a very useful toolkit and in this sense it is a means to an end but not necessarily an end in itself. There are many other 'means' out there, including a vast world of psychology, management theory and personal development.

In this book you will find influences from many places; however, we have endeavoured to keep this volume relatively theory light. There are plenty of models dotted about the book, but each of them is a framework for planning and doing; for preparing and delivering. This is not designed to be an academic book; it is not *about* our research... it is designed to be the *result* of our research... the *how to*! In addition, this is not a book *about* NLP, but it is a *result* of using NLP... and it is as practical as we can make it.

The Model Presenter

Our 20 Year 'Modelling Project'

As trainers ourselves, over the past twenty years we have been fascinated by what makes an excellent trainer (and presenter) versus what makes a mediocre or poor one. What is the difference? What engages an audience and what does not?

This has been what we would call an 'informal' modelling project, where we have observed hundreds of people in action, keeping notes about what works and what doesn't. During that time we have been teaching these models and skills to others via 'Presentation Skills' and 'Train the Trainer' courses, testing out the concepts as we went along.

We focussed mainly on the behaviour of others and on the 'mind set' of ourselves. Some of the 'mind set' was also elicited from others through conversation and questions. According to Robert Dilts'[1] definitions, the type of modelling we used would be called 'macro' modelling.

Whilst this is approximate, our 'population' for study consisted of:
- Observing, videoing, taking notes and giving feedback to about 1500 people on our presentation/train the trainer courses. About 750 hours.
- Experiencing and taking notes from approximately 100 speakers and presenters live, e.g. teaching workshops, giving talks or speaking at conferences. About 3000 hours.
- Watching videos, listening to audio recordings and taking notes of presenters and trainers running seminars and workshops. About 1000 hours.
- Listening to audio recordings of ourselves with a focus on voice and language use. About 200 hours.

Notes & Further Reading

Chapter 2
1. Cialdini, R. (2007) *Influence: The Psychology of Persuasion*, Harper Business
2. Janis, I. (1982) *Groupthink* Houghton Mifflin

Chapter 3
1. Maslow (1997) *Motivation and Personality*, Pearson
2. Herzberg, F. (1993) *Motivation to Work* Transaction Publishers

Chapter 6
1. David Kolb developed the Experiential Learning Model in the 1970s. It appears that he himself was inspired by the works of psychologists Jean Piaget, Kurt Lewin and, arguably, Carl Jung and Carl Rogers.
2. Peter Honey and Alan Mumford developed an 80 question Learning Styles questionnaire.
3. Bernice McCarthy has written numerous books on the 4Mat system including: *About Learning* and *Teachiong Around the 4Mat Cycle*.
4. There are a range of activity books for trainers, including *Games Trainers Play* by Edward Scannell and John Newstrom.

Chapter 7
1. Mehrabian, A. (2007) *Nonverbal Communication*, Aldine Transaction

Chapter 8
1. The website in question (accessed 23/06/13) was:
    http://www.computationalscience.org/ccce/Lesson2/Noteboo
    k%202%20Lecture.pdf
2. From an article: "How Language shapes thought" by Lera
    Boroditsky, Stanford University, based on some of her own
    research. (in *Scientific American*, Feb 2011, v304no2.
3. Sensory language (known in Neuro-linguistic programming
    as 'predicates') is explored in Bandler, R., & Grinder, J. T.
    (1976). *The Structure of Magic II*. Palo Alto, Calif.: Science and
    Behavior Books.
4. This is also known as 'switching referential index'. The
    referential index is 'who' is being referred to.
5. 'Gifting' is a term used by John Overdurf and Julie
    Silverthorn. Their book *Training Trances* is an excellent guide
    to bringing a difference into your training approach.

Chapter 9
1. The *Chicken Soup for the Soul* series of books are by Jack
    Canfield and Mark Victor Hanson. They contain heart
    warming stories of people facing adversity. There are lots of
    other books about and containing metaphors and short
    stories, for example: *Therapeutic Metaphors* by David Gordon,
    Magic of Metaphor by Nick Owen and *I Is an Other* by James
    Geary.

Chapter 10
1. For further discussion of Erickson's pacing & leading, see:
    Bandler, R. & Grinder, J. (1975). *Patterns of the hypnotic
    techniques of Milton H Erickson, M.D. (Vol. 1)*. Meta
    Publications.

Chapter 11
1. For further discussion of Erickson's 'artfully vague'
    language patterns, see: Bandler, R. & Grinder, J. (1975).

Patterns of the hypnotic techniques of Milton H Erickson, M.D. (Vol. 1). Meta Publications
2. Doodling reference: Article called "Superdoodles" by Catherine de Lange (*New Scientist* 22/29 December 2012 pp56-57)

Chapter 12
1. Bolte Taylor, J. (2009) *My Stroke of Insight* Hodder
2. Hall, L.M. (2012) *Meta-States* Neuro-Semantic Publications
3. It appears that 'ums' and 'ars' are actually useful for listeners in terms of helping them process and remember the content. For more information, see: (accessed 23/06/2013) http://www.apa.org/science/about/psa/2012/10/emphasis-gesture.aspx

Appendix 1
1. Dilts, R. (2006) *Modeling with NLP*, Meta Publications

About the Authors and
The GWiz Learning Partnership

About Joe Cheal

Joe is a partner in the GWiz Learning Partnership. He has been involved in the field of management and organisational development since 1993. In focusing his training, coaching and consultancy experience within the business environment, he has worked with a broad range of organisational cultures, helping thousands of people revolutionise the way they work with others.

He holds an MSc in Organisational Development and Neuro Linguistic Technologies (his MSc dissertation was an exploration into 'social paradox'), a degree in Philosophy and Psychology and diplomas in Coaching and Psychotherapy.

Joe is an NLP Master Trainer who enjoys learning new things... by exploring diverse fields of science, philosophy and psychology and then integrating these 'learnings'. He is the author of *Solving Impossible Problems* and is the creator and editor of the ANLP Journal: *Acuity*.

He is a regular speaker at conferences and groups. He can be contacted at: joe@gwiztraining.com.

About Melody Cheal

Melody has a degree in Psychology, a Masters Degree in Applied Positive Psychology, a diploma in Psychotherapy and is a Certified NLP Master Trainer. She is a member of the external verification panel for the ANLP accreditation programme.

She is also a qualified Myers Briggs practitioner and EI practitioner and has had five years Transactional Analysis training, meaning she is able to help organisations access the hidden potential in their staff. She is also in demand for her work in transforming average or even troubled teams into high performers.

As a partner in The GWiz Learning Partnership, Melody runs courses in both the private and the public sector, focusing on interpersonal skills and self-awareness. Over the last twenty years she has worked with international committees, directors, senior managers, teams and front line staff in groups and one to one as a coach. She is also an ILM accredited trainer.

She can be contacted at: melody@gwiznlp.com.

The GWiz Learning Partnership

The GWiz Learning Partnership is a consultancy that specialises in inspiring the natural potential of organisations, leadership, management and individuals through OD, L&D and Executive Coaching.

We work with clients from a broad range of sectors and aim to work in partnership with our clients, enhancing the profile of leadership, learning and development in our client's organisation.

Since 1993 we have experience of working with thousands of people from many organisations including:

Aeroflex, Amnesty International, ARA (Aircraft Research Association), Astra Zeneca & AstraTech, Autoglass, Balfour Beatty, Bedford Borough Council, Central Bedfordshire, Beds Health, Beds Magistrates Courts Committee, Belron, Bio-Products Laboratories (BPL), Birdlife and Plantlife, British Gas, BT, Calderdale Council, Cambridge City Council,

Cambridge University Press, Camelot, Cellnet, Central Bedfordshire, Cranfield University, Dixons Stores Group International, Emmaus Village Carlton, GSK, Herts Magistrates Courts Committee, Hertsmere Borough Council, Inland Revenue, Langley Search & Selection, Lockheed Martin, London Borough of Camden, Luton Borough Council, Mylan, NewhamCouncil, North Herts District Council, OAG, Olympic Blinds, RSPB, Sainsbury's, Serco, Shepherd Stubbs Recruitment, Staverton Park Conference Centre, The Assessment Network, Tesco, Welwyn Hatfield Borough Council, Willmott Dixon, The Wine Society.

The GWiz Learning Partnership offers a range of consultancy services including:

- Change management, OD and L&D consultancy
- Courses
- Executive coaching and skills coaching
- Facilitation
- Team development
- Myers Briggs profiling and Emotional Intelligence testing
- ILM accredited qualifications
- Qualifications in NLP
- GWizzlers ('bite-size' sessions)

Our courses and topics include:

LEADERSHIP DEVELOPMENT	PERSONAL IMPACT
Change Management	Career & Profile Development
Coaching Performance	Coping with Change
Coaching Skills for Managers	Dealing With Pressure
The Complete Leader: Inspirational & Practical	Innovation: Getting Creative
Delegate!	Lift Off: Personal Development
Feedback for Effectiveness	Making Your Life Work 4U: Confidence
Leadership in Action	Managing Your Performance
Making Meetings Work	Networking Skills
Management Development Programme	Personal Power
Managing Home-Workers	Self Awareness & Personal Development
Managing People Successfully	Staying Positively Happy
Mentoring 1: Becoming a Mentor	Stress Management
Mentoring 2: Developing Further Mentor Skills	Time Management

Motivate!
Project Leadership
The Supportive Manager
Team Building and Development

RESULTS AND RELATIONSHIPS
Advanced Customer Care
Assertiveness: Clarity and Focus
Building Partnerships
Communication
Conflict Resolution
Customer Care
Dealing with Aggression
Dealing with Difficult People
Handling Conflict in Meetings
Influence and Persuasion
Listening Completely
Magic of Mediation
Negotiation Skills
Rapport
Understanding Personalities

IN FRONT OF THE AUDIENCE
Advanced Presentation Skills
The Essential Presenter
Persuasive Presentations
Train the Trainer

EXECUTIVE DEVELOPMENT
Advanced Negotiation Skills
Becoming a Mentor
Beyond Selling
Business Hypnotix
Executive Leadership in Action
Making NLP Work
Managing Tensions
Organisational Development
Organisational Politics
Storytelling in Business
Strategic Change Management
Troubleshooting: Problem Resolution
Working with Transactional Analysis

HR SKILLS FOR MANAGERS
Appraisal
Capability & Disciplinary
Controlling Absence
Dealing with Poor Performance
Introduction to Counselling
Managing Difficult People
Recruitment Selection & Interviewing
Tackling Bullying & Harassment

CPD FOR HR PROFESSIONALS
Building Working Partnerships
Influencing the Organisation
Raising the Profile of HR

Have a look at our website: www.gwiztraining.com or contact us at info@gwiztraining.com.

Training in Neuro-linguistic Programming (NLP)

NLP (Neuro-linguistic Programming) could be described as the psychology of excellence and the science of change. Through understanding more about how the mind/brain works (neuro) and how language affects us (linguistic), a practitioner is able to initiate and sustain change (programming) on a personal, interpersonal and organisational level.

NLP was designed originally to model excellence. By establishing exactly how someone achieves something, excellence can be modelled, taught to someone else and repeated again and again. From this starting point, over the last thirty years, an array of processes, concepts and techniques have been developed to enable you to:

- become more resourceful in managing attitudes, thoughts, emotions, behaviours and beliefs
- relate to others easily and effortlessly,
- understand how language and its use has a direct impact on your state, your brain and your success in communicating with others.

In addition to all this, as a GWiz NLP practitioner, you will learn techniques designed to help you develop your own skills and help others develop theirs. The principles will be introduced conversationally and with activities throughout the course allowing you to learn on many levels consciously and unconsciously.

As NLP Master Trainers we offer the complete three levels of certified NLP courses throughout the year:

The Model Presenter

- NLP 101
- NLP Diploma
- NLP Practitioner
- NLP Master Practitioner
- NLP Trainer's Training

If you are interested in personal and professional development and would like to more about NLP, have a look at our website: www.gwiznlp.com or contact us: info@gwiznlp.com.